# FULCANELLI
## AND THE
## ALCHEMICAL REVIVAL

D1564775

# FULCANELLI
## AND THE
## ALCHEMICAL REVIVAL

## The Man behind the Mystery
## of the Cathedrals

### Geneviève Dubois

Translated by Jack Cain

Destiny Books
Rochester, Vermont

Destiny Books
One Park Street
Rochester, Vermont 05767
www.InnerTraditions.com

Destiny Books is a division of Inner Traditions International

Originally published in French under the title *Fulcanelli dévoilé* by Éditions
Dervy, 34, boulevard Edgar Quinet 75014, Paris
First U.S. edition published in 2006 by Destiny Books

**Library of Congress Cataloging-in-Publication Data**
Dubois, Geneviève.
  [Fulcanelli dévoilé. English]
  Fulcanelli and the alchemical revival : the man behind the Mystery of the cathe-
drals / Geneviève Dubois ; translated by Jack Cain.—1st U.S. ed.
      p. cm.
  Includes bibliographical references (p.      ).
  ISBN 1-59477-082-4 (pbk.)
  1. Fulcanelli, pseud. Mystère des cathédrals. 2. Alchemists—France—Biogra-
phy. 3. Alchemy—France—History. I. Title.
  QD24.A2D8313 2006
  540.1'12092--dc22
                                                            2005027427

Printed and bound in Canada by Transcontinental Printing

10  9  8  7  6  5  4  3  2  1

Text design and layout by Jon Desautels
This book was typeset in Sabon with Bank Gothic as the display typeface

*With thanks to*
*C. J. Faust,*
*Mrs. Duhamel,*
*the family of Pierre Dujols,*
*Mr. and Mrs. Daniel Finot,*
*and also, of course, the Saturday morning philosophers*

# CONTENTS

Copiapite

Essential oil

Vinegar

Glass

Talc

Subacetate of copper

# FOREWORD

If there is one enigma of our time that does not cease to pique the curiosity of seekers, and, moreover, which appears to be unsolvable, as is the case with famous historical mysteries such as Louis XVII and the Man in the Iron Mask, it is without a doubt the one occupying first place in the realm of hermetic science—that is, the haunting Fulcanelli affair.

Indeed, ever since the publication of the two famous works bearing this eloquent pseudonym, namely, *Le Mystère des Cathédrales* (1926)[1] and *Les Demeures Philosophales* (1930),[2] each subsequently republished twice, the attention of a certain segment of the public—the one generally limited in size but nevertheless attuned to the disciplines that have come to be known under the rubric of *esotericism,* understood to be a vast field in its own right—lost no time in becoming firmly fixated on the task of identifying the real author of these books, without, however, managing to puncture the facade of anonymity that has seemed impervious to all attack.

The attempts at solving the mystery of Fulcanelli's identity have been many. Even foreign countries, notably Spain, have been involved, without, in the end, any solution being found. Various specialized journals have published serious articles bearing on this irksome question, but the mystery has remained intact, to the great disappointment of all those who have hoped for a solution.

Before proceeding further on the topic of Fulcanelli, however, I believe that it is of paramount importance to dispel in advance any ambiguity as to the true nature of alchemy, a subject so maligned and adapted to any purpose that anyone at all, no matter his qualifications, has felt free to offer an explanation of the meaning of this high science. Thus we hear talk of such things as "spiritual alchemy" and "Tantric alchemy" when we are not seeing alchemy saddled with psychoanalytical meanings by a certain school that is attached to psychic archetypes, notably those arising from the study of dreams and taking as their subject matter the study of man! All these erroneous conceptions seem to arise for some individuals entirely from the results of a total misunderstanding of the Sacred Art, whereas for others, these misunderstandings seem to come from a deliberate willfulness to lead minds astray.

It should also be noted that in many works with alchemical aspirations, the authors, lacking adequate information, commit the common and unacceptable mistake of claiming a supposed "Black Work" that foreshadows, as they would say, two following stages designated, respectively, the "White Work" and the "Red Work."

The truth of the matter is that these two "final" stages, which lead to real but different results, constitute *within themselves alone* the core of the hermetic work, the black representing only what the alchemists mean by "putrefaction."

In reality, it is quite clear that even though it absolutely cannot be thought of apart from its fiery oven, authentic alchemy is something entirely other. And in order to defer to three authors who are duly qualified and whose authority in this matter is unanimously recognized in hermetic circles, I cannot resist the salutary obligation of transcribing their respective advice, starting with my old friend of forty years, Eugène Canseliet, the famous writer of prefaces for the two Fulcanelli works already mentioned, and who, in a manner not unpleasing to our omniscient scientists, declares forthrightly in his precious *Alchimie expliquée sur les textes classiques:* "How misguided it is that popular legend would have us believe that alchemy consists entirely in the artificial production of metallic gold when its principal goal is the discovery of the Universal Medicine that alone is the provider of the triple privilege of *knowledge, health,* and *wealth.*"³

Let us continue with these words from my very dear but recently departed friend Claude Lablatinière d'Ygé, who, in his *Nouvelle Assemblée des Philosophes Chymiques,* makes clear for us: "May those who think that alchemy is strictly of a character that is earthly, mineral, and metallic give it a wide berth. May those who think that alchemy is only a symbolism used to reveal through analogy the process of 'spiritual revelation'—in short, that man is the material and the athanor is his work—abandon it."⁴

Here is a clearly stated extract from the fifth "Épistola Hermetica," published in the highly regarded journal *Atlantis,* founded by Paul Le Cour:

> Yes, there exists in fact only one alchemy that is not so much ours as that of Nicolas Flamel and that of Basile Valentin, the Cosmopolite, Cyliani, or Fulcanelli. . . . How terribly crude it is seen to be—this idea often encountered that holds that alchemy is solely the wild pursuit of the ancient Chrysopoeia,* as if men of the past, just as those in this age of iron, had been only hateful materialists greedy for riches before all else, without the slightest concern for the *welfare of their souls*! The ultimate goal of the alchemical quest, far and away beyond all other goals, consists in this: to help the person—one who is in no way a mystic—to establish his welfare while on this earth, just as such a person, leaning over the crucible, helps the raw material to be purified until the "Light of the Light" (that is, the *Lumen de Lumine* of the Nicene Creed of the year 325) is obtained.⁵

Could anything be more explicit than these three incontrovertible declarations? Such statements are quite necessary in order to place those "Lovers of Science," who are sincere but are just beginning on

*[The term *chrysopoeia* is sometimes used to refer to the whole process of the transmutation of base metals into gold. —*Trans.*]

their guard against widely distributed and terrible books that can do nothing but lead us down the garden path. What is also indicated by this is how we must strictly follow only those texts recognized as classic texts!

Now let us return to the purpose of this preface: describing the recent situation concerning the mysterious pseudonym Fulcanelli.

And it was just then, with benevolent concern, that Providence, judging no doubt that the moment had come to have the truth burst forth, descended upon a young woman who had always been haunted by this mystery and who was a member of our little spiritualist group in Grenoble. Fascinated by this famous enigma, Geneviève Dubois, for it is indeed she we are speaking of, firmly rose to the challenge by adopting the unshakable resolution to try and tear away the veil.

Embodying a limitless energy together with a tenacity and discernment worthy of Sherlock Holmes, she did not hesitate to mobilize all resources to reach her goal, exemplifying thereby the famous saying: "What woman wants, God wants."

Not stinting on the inevitable expenses that such an inquiry involves, our friend took many trips and established numerous and fruitful contacts, both in the provinces, in areas sometimes very distant from one another, and particularly in Paris, where sharp minds, won over by her endeavor, were quick to offer her their bibliographic skills and their support. Without letting herself become disconcerted by the scope and extreme difficulty of the task, our intuitive investigator managed fortuitously to meet certain involved families who, convinced of the sincerity of her undertaking, freely made available their textual and visual archives, going so far as to authorize the making of copies and photographic reproductions, a large number of which appear in this publication.

In conclusion, I consider it a duty to pay well-deserved homage to Geneviève Dubois, for her book, embellished with a lively style that is inlaid at times with felicitous turns of phrase, provides a very developed and ever-so-revealing synthesis that forms the crowning glory of all the efforts undertaken to arrive, finally and happily, at the conclusion of such a thankless, complex, and incredible inquiry.

Refusing to give away anything, even in part, concerning her work, and wanting not to overly tax the patience of the reader, I am anxious to let the author lead on from one surprise to the next.

May this revelatory book enjoy the widest possible audience. That is the wish that is forming in my heart of hearts in concluding this humble preface for which Geneviève Dubois so kindly sought me out and which I have taken such pleasure in providing, despite my limited qualifications, because of our already long-standing, loyal, and solid friendship.

*Felix qui potuit rerum cognoscere causas.**

VIRGIL, GEORGICS, 2:489

ROGER GALLOIS, SIMPLE CHILD OF THE SCIENCE

---

*["Happy is he who can understand the causes of things." —*Trans.*]

*Part 1*

# BACKGROUND

# 1

# THE CHAIN OF HERMES, OR THE PERSISTENCE OF THE SCIENCE OF ALCHEMY

Toward the middle of the nineteenth century, groups of occultists appeared that were characterized by their attempts, using metaphysical speculation and experiments that today would be termed paranormal, to validate the idea of survival after death and to give a meaning to life.

Europe was following the path of symbolism and meditation. In this, people were reacting to the positivism of Auguste Comte. This philosophy, developed between 1830 and 1842, countering romantic lyricism and influenced by the progress of the biological sciences, held that it was necessary to limit knowledge to truths based on observation and experiment and to abandon the attempt to know the essence of things.

It was then that there arose movements such as the spiritualism of Allan Kardec; Theosophy, which drew its inspiration from the Far East; and the Anthroposophism of Rudolf Steiner, which are among the best known.

It should be noted that at the end of the eighteenth century and at the beginning of the nineteenth, the Encyclopedists tried to pull back from religious dogma, and the most eminent thinkers put forth the idea of conducting research separate from faith. For example, one of these, Swedenborg, maintained that he had attained mystical experience as a result of science.

Alchemy in this period appeared to have become obsolete. Its doctrine—as was the case, moreover, with the so-called occult sciences—had been dismissed since the second half of the seventeenth century with Descartes. It seemed to have completely disappeared with the triumph of the chemistry of Lavoisier, for he proclaimed that a simple substance is indecomposable, a theory incompatible with the alchemical credo, which holds the opposite to be the case. The famous chemist meant to put an end to beliefs about the possibilities of transmutation. Science thus entertained the hope of penetrating the mysteries of nature.

The century was not, however, so dismal as we might be led to believe. Some scholars appeared on the scene—Dom Pernety[1] and his *Fables Égyptiennes et Grecques;* Joseph Balsamo, known as Cagliostro; Count St. Germain*; Abbé Nicolas Lenglet-Dufresnoy;[2] and the famous Alliette,[3] under his pseudonym Etteila (nearly an anagram of his name)—who left us three interesting treatises together with a Tarot. Isolated and in secret, some alchemists continued to search for the philosopher's stone.

One name that stands out clearly in the second half of the eighteenth century is James Price, the English doctor and chemist and member of the Royal Society. He made chemical discoveries and worked as an

---

*Count St. Germain, *La Très Sainte-Trinosophie* (Paris: Retz, 1971); from a manuscript preserved at the Troyes library (no. 2,400, in quarto, ninety-nine leaves written in a fine hand, twelve figures, twenty-four painted vignettes, and seven philosophical and magical figures made up of Hebrew letters).

At the top of the work are two notes. The first is signed "J. B. C. Philotaume" and certifies that "this manuscript is the only existing copy of the famous trinosophy of Count St. Germain, which he himself destroyed on one of his journeys." The second note, unsigned, tells us that "this unusual manuscript is that which belonged to the famous Cagliostro and which was recovered by Masséna among the papers of the Grand Inquisitor." See Marie-Raymonde Delorme, *Le Comte Saint-Germain* (Loisirs: Culture, Art, 1973).

alchemist in his private laboratory, obtaining a powder that transmuted mercury and silver into gold. Beginning in 1782, according to Sadoul, he performed public transmutations in the village of Gilford, where he had bought a manor. His end was tragic: Convinced that he would be taken for an impostor, he committed suicide.

Curiosity was sustained and awakened by authors such as Goethe, born in 1749, who took a genuine interest in Hermeticism, the transmission of which he ensured. His *Faust* is an icon of esotericism. Nineteenth-century romantic literature seized upon the image of the alchemist, perverting it by promoting the antiquated image of a solitary and cursed magician. In 1831, Gérard de Nerval wrote *Nicolas Flamel,* and in 1838 Alexandre Dumas wrote a piece called "L'Alchimiste." Finally, also in 1831, Victor Hugo published his famous novel *Notre-Dame-de-Paris.*

A year later, in 1832, a little anonymous tract[4] appeared under the title *Hermès Dévoilé, dédié à la Postérité,*[5] published by Félix Locquin in Paris, at 16 rue Notre-Dame-des-Victoires. The author signed his work "Ci . . ." at the end. He stated that he had obtained what he had been seeking after numerous false starts and after so many years: the elucidation of the alchemical Great Work. This book was considered, first by Fulcanelli and then by Eugène Canseliet, as the story of an adept whose word could be trusted. It is true that this text, so touching in its enumeration of the misfortunes that befell this hermeticist, reveals a real mastery of the wet way and an acquaintance with exterior influences. Canseliet and Fulcanelli refer to it frequently.

In July of 1843, another Frenchman made known his deep interest in the science of Hermes: Louis-Paul-François Cambriel[6] was seventy-nine years old at the time of the appearance of his nineteen-lesson course on the practice of the Great Work. In June of 1819, he had included in the "petites affiches"* an offer of "great benefit" asking for financial help in order to bring his research to fruition. He proposed very rewarding conditions for repayment.

---

*[Small personal advertisements. —*Trans.*]

The chemist Chevreul criticized him very bluntly in a series of four articles that appeared in *Le Journal des Savants* beginning in May 1851. Chevreul had assembled one of the most extensive libraries of old alchemical manuscripts, which he left to the Muséum d'Histoire Naturelle in Paris (Chevreul Collection). Then, in 1844, a small book by Alexandre Dumas, *Un Alchimiste au XIXe siècle,* was printed in Paris. This book dealt with a friend of the author's, Viscount Henri de Ruolz, who was of German origin but whose family had lived in France for three centuries.

A doctor of law and of medicine, Ruolz's sole passions were music and chemistry. Though he opted for medicine, he actually began conducting alchemical experiments. In doing this he connected with two of his friends: Albert Charles Ernest Franquet de Franqueville, of the graduating class of 1827, who worked for the roads department, and Frantz de Mont-Richer.

Henri de Ruolz and Mont-Richer tried to make diamonds rather than gold, and they succeeded. The great-nephew of Franqueville, Dubreton (École Polytechnique 1901), affirms that Alexandre Dumas's story is reliable.

During the same period, in 1850, there was published in England a curious book written by Mary Anne Atwood (maiden name: South) and entitled *A Suggestive Inquiry into the Hermetic Mystery*. Her father was a scholar of classical and medieval philosophy.

She studied Latin and Greek as an aid in drawing up a classification index for ancient knowledge. First, she published an anonymous essay that caused quite a stir in esoteric circles: "Early Magnetism in Its Higher Relations to Humanity as Veiled in the Poets and the Prophets." At the age of thirty-seven, her book on alchemy was presented to the public. More than one hundred copies had been sold when, with the assistance of her father, she set up a bonfire on the lawn of their house in Gosport in order to burn the remaining books as well as those already sold that she was able to retrieve. A few copies, however, must have escaped, for in 1918, an edition from W. Tait appeared with a preface by W. L. Wilmshurst. This edition was reprinted in 1960 in New York by the Julian Press.

Mary Anne Atwood died in 1910 at the age of ninety-seven, having never spoken of this affair.

# 2
# THE TENOR OF THE TIMES

We shall now enter the era into which the works of Fulcanelli thrust their roots: the domain of occultists and Freemasonry at the end of the nineteenth century and the beginning of the twentieth century. Names introduced in italics are those of individuals who have a link to the Fulcanelli mystery.*

The creation of numerous groups studying the esoteric sciences, along with their meeting places, meetings, and press publications, fostered the blossoming of an abundant literature. Individuals from all social classes who shared a similar enthusiasm were able to work side by side. There was an amazing burgeoning of ideas in which alchemy played a leading part.

Strange characters appeared, studying in secret the art of Hermes. One among them, a shoemaker by trade, Rémi Pierret,†

---

*See appendix A for a complete chronology of all of the major figures in the story of the alchemical revival.

†It seems a manuscript copied in black, red, and green ink and signed "Rémi Pierret 1873" was found at the Bibliothèque Nationale, Paris. We looked for it in vain. It supposedly dealt with an interesting "Collection of Alchemical Procedures" and contained among other things numerous alchemical experiments using "Nostoc or *flos coeli*." At the end there was a recipe for "potable gold" extracted from a manuscript written in 1744 and two pen-and-ink figures. Information culled from Dorbon-Aîné, *Bibliotheca Esoterica*, 89.

who occupied the concierge's quarters at 12 passage Ménilmontant, Paris, had assembled one of the most important alchemical libraries of the nineteenth century. The likes of *Papus,** Stanislas de Guaita, Albert Poisson, Victor-Émile Michelet, and Marc Haven† very often paid him visits in order to discuss with him the passionate interest they shared. But the indisputable master of this era was the gentleman from Lorraine, Stanislas de Guaita, who died in 1897 at age thirty-eight.

A copy of his work *La Clef de la Magie Noire* (The Key to Black Magic) that had belonged to *Jules Boucher* was annotated by Fulcanelli on the pages dealing with alchemy.[1] This information is given by Robert Amadou in his last article on the topic, entitled "L'Affaire Fulcanelli," that appeared in the journal *L'Autre Monde* (Another World). In fact, the annotations in question are reproduced in this article.

Albert Poisson‡ was an intimate friend of Stanislas de Guaita and had frequent exchanges with him. A bibliophile and a scholar, he became interested in alchemy at the age of twelve and browsed assidu-ously in used bookstores in order to uncover old treatises. He studied relentlessly during the morning in his apartment-laboratory on the rue Saint-Denis and in the afternoon earned his living at the laboratory of the Faculty of Medicine. Unfortunately, he was to die prematurely at the age of twenty-five, a victim of tuberculosis contracted in the army.

*Papus is the pseudonym of Dr. Encausse and the name of the medical genius that Encausse had found in the translation of the *Nuctemeron* of Apollonius of Tyana, from the Greek with a commentary by Eliphas Lévi.

†Marc Haven is the pseudonym of Dr. Emmanuel Lalande, son-in-law of the lawyer Philippe de Lyon, thaumaturgist.

‡Albert Poisson, *Théorie et Symbole des Alchimistes* (Paris: Éditions Chacornac, 1891). He left his library to Papus and Marc Haven. He was most certainly a pupil of Rémi Pierret, the shoemaker-cum-alchemist who had a career in Freemasonry.

In the *Voile d'Isis*, Albert Poisson signed an article—"L'Alchimie à l'Institut," relating the experiences of the American alchemist Carey Lea—with the pseudonym Philophotes (see *Voile d'Isis*, no. 69).

In no. 71 of the same journal, he wrote an article on alchemy and in no. 72 another on prophetic dreams. Within the Groupe Indépendant d'Études Ésotériques (Independent Group for Esoteric Studies), he founded an alchemical school based on experiments in the laboratory.

In 1888, Stanislas de Guaita, with the help of Papus and Joséphin Péladan, decided to establish a new, so-called kabbalistic, Rosicrucian order of which the Supreme Council was to include six known members and six hidden members. The grand master was Guaita; Barlet* and Papus subsequently replaced him. Oswald Wirth,[2] Lucien Lejay, and Paul Adam also belonged to the group, and later, Marc Haven, Augustin Chaboseau, and Sédir† (who resigned in 1909) were associated with it.

After two years, Joséphin Péladan separated from Papus and Guaita to form the Esthetic and Catholic Rosicrucian Order, a sort of intellectual Tiers-Ordre.‡ This movement was to attract a whole group of painters, writers, and musicians; among those who joined were Erik Satie; Alfred Jarry, who, influenced by hermetic symbolism, would allow his convictions to show through in his works; Count A. de la Rochefoucauld; Gary de Lacroze; and Saint-Pol-Roux.

Beginning in 1923, Joséphin Péladan further organized six Rosicrucian salons attended by Gauguin, Zola, and Verlaine. His initiative proved fortunate, for it helped to make known these artists and writers who subsequently became famous.

As for Papus, it is clear that he was very active in esoteric circles during these years. He was familiar with the artistic high society of Paris and was a regular at the Chat Noir cabaret, which had been established and run by Rodolphe Salis and about whose sign Fulcanelli made an interesting comment in *The Dwellings of the Philosophers*.[3]

There Papus was to meet *Ferdinand de Lesseps*, Augusta Holmes, and the singer Emma Calvé, whose name is forever linked to the disturbing story of Rennes-le-Château. The first two were keenly interested in esotericism and participated actively in spiritualistic séances. We will

---

*F. Ch. Barlet is the pseudonym of Albert Faucheux. The name Barlet is an anagram of Albert.

†Sédir is the pseudonym of Yvon Le Loup.

‡[Tiers-Ordre (Third Order) is a term used to denote an association of devout adherents of the Catholic Church who, although they live in the world, are associated with a religious order. —*Trans.*]

see later how the name Emma Calvé can be shown to be connected to that of Fulcanelli.

Among Papus's contacts was Anatole France, who ran a glossy journal to which Maurice Barrès and Victor-Émile Michelet contributed. It was through this journal that Papus was able to be in touch with Anatole France. For his part, France, in putting together his novel *La Rôtisserie de la Reine Pédauque,* borrowed complete pages from Montfaucon de Villars's work *Le Comte de Gabalis.*[4]

Every Wednesday in Paris, society figures gathered at the home of the countess Gaston d'Adhémar. Among them could be found Papus,* Joséphin Péladan, the bookstore proprietor Edmond Bailly, Gary de Lacroze, and many others. Starting in 1889, all these figures of the artistic high society of Paris went to dine every Thursday at the home of Georges Poirel, developer of a phototype process, on the rue de la Tour-d'Auvergne. Besides Papus, de Guaita, and Péladan, other invitees were Oswald Wirth, Émile Goudeau,[†] and Édouard Schuré. Ideas were exchanged and

---

*At the time, Papus was engaged in the study of medicine and was carrying out his military service. He had been drawn to alchemy by reading the works of Louis Lucas: *La Chimie Nouvelle* (The New Chemistry), 1854; *Le Roman Alchimique* (The Alchemical Novel), the publication of which began in no. 14 of the *Voile d'Isis* and later appeared in 1857 as a book; and *La Médecine Nouvelle* (The New Medicine), 1862.

†Émile Goudeau was the founder of Les Hydropathes. His major work is *La Revanche des Bêtes* (The Revenge of the Beasts).

The launching of the cabaret Le Chat Noir in Montmartre arose from the meeting of the painter Rodolphe Salis and Émile Goudeau. The latter had created a poetry circle, Les Hydropathes, to which singers and poets came to drink and exchange ideas about their work. Meetings took place at the Soleil d'Or on the boulevard Saint-Michel. During the same period, a thin, ghostly poet from Picardy settled in at 84 boulevard Rochechouart, where he transformed a former postal substation into a workshop and a factory for the production of religious paintings. Now, it happened that one evening Émile Goudeau stopped at the Grande Pinte. After he had been there a few moments, a lively troupe burst in. In this group were the painter Gilbert and Léon Valade. Gilbert pointed out to his friend Goudeau a young man among them who was about to open an artists cabaret at 84 boulevard Rochechouart. This young man, named Rodolphe Salis, invited Émile Goudeau to the inaugural dinner and when, at this opening event, he saw all these artists and writers gathered, he understood the advantage that he could draw from it. Thus, with a black cat serving as its sign, the most prestigious cabaret of the era opened its doors in 1881. Details drawn from *Miroir de l'Histoire,* no. 206 (February 1967).

someone spoke of the latest publications on alchemy—for example, *Origines de l'Alchimie* by Berthelot, or possibly the work of Louis Figuier, the famous historian of this discipline.[5] Tiffereau also attracted attention; he was actually the leading figure in the field of alchemy.*

However, Georges Poirel left and settled in Brittany, where he eventually became a captain of long-range vessels.

Because they wanted to pursue these fruitful exchanges, the participants decided to form a group under the name Groupe Indépendant d'Études Ésotériques (Independent Group for Esoteric Studies). It began its functions on December 7, 1889, and continued until 1894, when it changed its name to the École Hermétique (Hermetic School).

The group included scholars, poets, artists, and writers. Among the best known, we can name Paul Adam, Victor-Émile Michelet, Péladan, Guaita, Poisson, Barlet, Lacroze, le Colonel de Rochas, Sédir, Marc Haven, Augustin Chaboseau, Phaneg, Doctor Rozier, Jollivet-Castelot, and Chamuel (Lucien Mauchel). At the urging of Papus and Villiers de l'Isle-Adam, Chamuel opened a shop as well as a library at the sign of the Librairie du Merveilleux (Bookstore of the Marvelous), 29 rue de Trévise, and, in the same street a little farther along, a room where lectures were held every week.

In 1888 Papus started the journal *L'Initiation*.† He was twenty-three years old. All the leading figures of the era wrote for it. This journal continued until 1912 and in 1891 was placed on the index [of forbidden books] by the Catholic Church. In 1890, Papus also began the *Voile d'Isis*, the mouthpiece of the Groupe Indépendant d'Études Ésotériques. Grillot de Givry[6] was one of his collaborators. The first issue appeared on November 12, 1890; the editor in chief was Augustin Chaboseau, Hidden Superior, and the secretary was Lucien Mauchel (Chamuel). The *Voile d'Isis* was later named *Les Études Traditionnelles.*

---

*Tiffereau, *L'Or et la Transmutation des Métaux* (Gold and the Transmutation of Metals, Paris: n.p., n.d.). The transmutation that he carried out in Mexico in 1842 caused a stir in all sectors of the society of those times.

†An independent philosophical journal of advanced studies, hypnotism, Theosophy, Kabbalah, Freemasonry, and occult sciences.

Various groups belonged to the Groupe Indépendant d'Études Ésotériques, one of which was the École Sociétaire which was founded by Fourier.

Concurrently, Papus laid the foundations of the Martinist movement, which enjoyed prodigious growth from 1890 to 1914 in most European countries. The Supreme Council was made up of Stanislas de Guaita, Maurice Barrès, and Péladan. These last two were replaced by Marc Haven and Victor-Émile Michelet. Paul Adam, F. Ch. Barlet, Chaboseau (then librarian of the Musée Guimet), Chamuel, Lejay, Montière, and Sédir were also members of this council. Papus was the president,[7] receiving an initiation from Henri Delage. The lineage was as follows: Louis-Claude de Saint-Martin, Antoine Chaptal, Henri Delage,* Papus. This lineage, which was subsequently contested, is given by Jean-Marie Parent and Roger Facon in *Sectes et Sociétés Secrètes aujourd'hui . . .* (Sects and Secret Societies Today . . .).[8]

The members of the Martinist association met at the bookstore of the occultist Edmond Bailly, whose shop on the rue de la Chaussée-d'Antin, marked by the sign l'Art Indépendant, was frequented by both those from the Symbolist Movement and those fascinated by esotericism. Edmond Bailly published the journals *La Haute Science* (The High Science) and *L'Étoile* (The Star); Jules Bois, the editor of these journals, was the lover of the singer Emma Calvé.

Into this cozy retreat thronged writers such as Huysmans, Mallarmé, Villiers de l'Isle-Adam, Félicien Rops, the painter Odilon Redon, Henri de Reigner, Pierre Louÿs, and the musicians Debussy, Erik Satie, and many others. In his book *Les Compagnons de la Hiérophanie* (The Fellows of Hierophancy), Victor-Émile Michelet describes for us a number of these figures.

The accredited students of the École Hermétique (formerly the Groupe Indépendant d'Études Ésotériques) entered Martinist lodges

---

*Henri Delage was born in 1825 and died in 1882 and is the author of numerous books, among them *Initiation au magnétisme* (Initiation to Magnetism), 1847, and *Doctrine des Sociétés Secrètes* (Doctrine of Secret Societies), 1852.

called le Sphynx, la Sphynge, Hermanubus, and Véléda. Martinism was supposed to have been the antechamber of a much older order, the H.B. of Luxor (Hermetic Brotherhood of Luxor). In fact, this turned out not to be the case, and the Kabbalistic Rosicrucian Order became the inner circle. The route then became: École Hermétique to Martinism to the Kabbalistic Rosicrucian Order. After the death of its founder, Stanislas de Guaita, it was F. Ch. Barlet who became the grand master. When he resigned, Papus claimed to be the successor to Barlet and therefore grand master of the order, whereas Barlet had passed on the title and the archives to *René Guénon.*[9]

F. Ch. Barlet (1838–1921) was the official representative in France of the H.B. of L. It was an extremely secretive fraternity revived around 1870. Peter Davidson was one of the leaders and Max Théon, a strange individual, was the adept.[10] The H.B. of Luxor was the outer shell of a very old center of initiation. Close to thirty thousand intellectuals were affiliated with the brotherhood, one of whom was Abraham Lincoln. Members could be found in Scotland, Egypt, and America. The teaching related to a practice intended to develop spiritual faculties and was based on the theories and practices of P. B. Randolph, author of the well-known *Magia Sexualis.*[11]

Serge Hutin assures us in his book *Paul Sédir, Histoire des Rose-Croix* (Paul Sédir: History of the Rosicrucians) that Randolph was a member of this fraternity, and Pierre Mariel, in his *Dictionnaire des Sociétés Secrètes* (Dictionary of Secret Societies), notes that Papus, Chaboseau, and Marc Haven were as well.

But let us return to the École Hermétique (formerly Groupe Indépendant d'Études Ésotériques), which ran courses four times a week at 13 rue Séguier. Many people took these courses. The proceedings were conducted by F. Ch. Barlet, Papus, Sédir, Phaneg, and so forth, and among the students was Jollivet-Castelot, who met most of the occultists of his time this way. He joined the Martinist Society.

In his largely autobiographical book, *Le Destin* (Destiny), he competently describes the most famous figures of the 1890s. Papus is described as "jovial, cordial, with a somewhat common exterior and an untidy appearance . . . occupying lodgings at Auteuil, Villa Montmorency."

Sédir was seen as "an often arcane lecturer, looking down on his listeners, living in a garret on the avenue de l'Opéra." Guaita is described as being "thickset, authoritarian, disdainful of the commonplace." Also, we learn that Saint-Yves d'Alveydre lived "in a sumptuous residence in Versailles, peaceful and furnished luxuriously. He received visitors in a little salon adjacent to his study; he spoke quietly and well and dressed in purple velvet."

In 1896, Jollivet-Castelot formed the Société Alchimique de France and launched the journal *L'Hyperchimie*—a monthly journal of alchemy, hermetic science, and spagyric medicine. It appeared regularly for about ten years. Sédir was the editor in chief and Jollivet-Castelot the director. In 1904 it was revamped and took the name *Nouveaux Horizons de la Science et de la Pensée* (New Horizons in Science and Thought); it continued to be published until 1914. After 1920, it became *La Rose-Croix* (The Rosy Cross). In 1939, Jollivet-Castelot died at Douai after having generated a great deal of press due to his experiments with transmutation and the making of gold. The recipe was generously revealed in his journal, and an engineer from Lyons successfully repeated his experiments. Jollivet-Castelot, the "hyperchemist," left us several publications, including *Comment On devient alchimiste* (How One Becomes an Alchemist) in 1897 and in 1901, *La Science alchimiste* (The Science of Alchemy).

During the same period, in 1898, a Spaniard, Antonio de Paula Novellas y Roig, published the text of a lecture, "L'Alchimie et les Alchimistes" (Alchemy and the Alchemists), that he had delivered to the Groupe Scolaire Raymond Lulle[12] in Barcelona. He professed to be passionate about spagyric methods, notably a preparation called La Thériaque* He was an astonishing man who frequented the scientific circles of his time and professed theories derived from the ancient hermetic tradition.

---

*[A *theriac* is a cure-all or antidote to a poison. —*Ed.*]

We will now sketch the connections that *René Guénon* maintained with these esoteric circles and show the close ties that linked him to the small group in which the works signed "Fulcanelli" were developed.

At the beginning of 1908, René Guénon, who was taking courses at the École Hermétique that were given by Papus and his friends, joined the Martinist Order.

Some younger members met at a hotel at 17 rue des Canettes in Paris. They practiced automatic writing, and a certain Jean Desjobert acted as a medium. This little group was noteworthy by the presence at its core of *Lucien Faugeron,* disciple in hermetic science of *Pierre Dujols;* and *Alexandre Thomas,* the associate of the same Pierre Dujols at the Librairie du Merveilleux.

During a séance, the pseudo-entity who spoke through the medium Desjobert gave the order to bring René Guénon to the next séance. He came and was exhorted to create an Ordre du Temple Rénové (Order of the Temple Renewed) of which he was to be the head. The "spirits" who manifested during this period were: Cagliostro, Jacques de Molay,* Frederick the Great, and Weishaupt. High society indeed!

On February 23, 1908, the ritual of this new Ordre du Temple was laid down with seven grades and twelve members. The founding of this movement finalized the break between Guénon and Papus, who excluded Guénon from his groups. But in 1911, the "masters" who controlled the medium ordered René Guénon to dissolve the order. This was done. According to André Gilis,[13] this ephemeral revival of the Ordre du Temple was the privileged ground from which the work of Guénon sprang forth.

A related influence was the mediumistic séances of the Mouvement Cosmique, founded in 1900 by Max Théon after the disbanding of the H.B. of L (1887–88). F. Ch. Barlet supported the diffusion of the ideas coming from this movement by means of meetings and a journal called

---

*[The last grand master of the Knights Templar, burned as a heretic in 1314. —*Ed.*]

*La Revue Cosmique.* Well-known people worked hard to support this organization. Among them were Anna de Noailles, Édouard Schuré, the Hellenist Mario Meunier, and Dr. Serge Voronoff, who was connected to *Jean-Julien Champagne* by an incident recounted by Robert Ambelain, which we will speak about again later. The editorial secretary of the *La Revue Cosmique* was Julien Lejay, a well-known Martinist.

Max Théon, founder of the Mouvement Cosmique and an adept of the defunct H.B. of Luxor, traveled to France in 1888 and to Paris in 1920. He claimed to be an initiate who had achieved earthly immortality, and he seemed to possess numerous powers. From a state of contemplation, his wife, an Irish poetess, wrote the texts of the Cosmic Philosophy. She died in 1908 during a trip to Jersey. Max Théon lived until 1926, the year of his death, at Tlemcen, in Algeria. According to Pierre Geyraud, "the guardian of Cosmic Philosophy originated in Tunisia; his name, Aia Aziz, was often replaced in the *Revue Cosmique* by his emblem, a lotus."[14]

In 1911, René Guénon entered the Thébah Lodge of the Grand Lodge of France, conforming to the Ancient and Accepted Scottish Rite. He had been refused by the lodge called Travail et Vrais Amis Fidèles (Work and True Faithful Friends). In 1917 at the latest, he ended his Masonic activities. At the same time, he applied for admission to the Église Gnostique (gnostic church), excommunicated by Rome, which was formed at the end of the nineteenth century by Jules Doinel, then directed by Fabre des Essarts (Synésius). The young Guénon, under the initiatory name Palingénius (with a homophonic wink to his given name: *rené = renaît = reborn*),* became its bishop in 1909.

---

*In Fulcanelli, *Les Demeures Philosophales,* volume 1, the chapter on the hermetic cabala ascribes to Palingenesia (referring to Marcel Palingène) the meaning of regeneration. "In order to designate the regeneration of the sun or of gold, using iron." [The translation maintains the distinction made in the French between the Hebrew Kabbalah and the species of esoteric wordplay and double entendre that is known as the phonetic or hermetic cabala. —*Ed.*]

Certain members of this church were very refined: Albert de Pouvourville (Matgioi), who was connected with Taoism, and Lucien Champrenaud, who was connected with Islam under the name Abdul-Haqq.

In November 1909, Guénon, still using the pseudonym Palingénius and in collaboration with others from the Ordre du Temple Rénové, notably A. Thomas (initiatory name: Marnès), created the journal *La Gnose* (Gnosis, 1909–12), published by the Librairie du Merveilleux, which was run by Pierre Dujols and Thomas. In 1928 he contributed to the Italian journal *Ignis*.

At the great Spiritualist and Masonic Conference of 1908, René Guénon was the office secretary and wore the silk cordon of Kadosh of the Swedenborgian Rite.*

Now we shall outline here the connections among the alchemists and thinkers of different countries.

In 1924 and 1927, two journals appeared in Italy, *Athanor* and *Ignis,* that were devoted to the exposition of initiatory doctrine. Arturo Reghini† directed them and contributed as well to the *Voile d'Isis*. It was

---

*The Swedenborgian Rite maintained close relations with Memphis-Misraïm Freemasonry. John Yarker was the grand master of the Supreme Grand Lodge of the Temple of the Swedenborgian Rite. As early as 1893 he had applied for admission to the inner circle of Martinism. At the time of la Belle Époque (1890–1914), we find some familiar faces connected to Jules Osselin at Memphis-Misraïm, among them Sédir, Marc Haven, Philippon, and the venerable Abel Thomas and his brother Albéric Alexandre, whom we know already as Paul Chacornac. Papus's application for admission was rejected under pressure from Abel Thomas.

Information drawn from Serge Caillet, *Franc-Maçonnerie Égyptienne de Memphis-Misraïm* (Paris, 1988).

†In the journal *Ignis* for 1925, Arturo Reghini provides a commentary on the text "Lux Obnubilata" (Light Moving Out from Darkness on Its Own) published in facsimile reproduction by Arché in Milan in 1968. The original edition is from 1666, published by Zatta, Venice. This text was published formerly in the journal *Nova Lux* and in the journal *Kremmezziana Commentarium* before appearing in *Ignis*. Arturo Reghini attributes the Ode to Philalèthe [Thomas Vaughan (1622–66), who wrote under the name Eugenius Philalethes].

he who introduced René Guénon to Julius Evola,* who was at the time head of the group called Ur, which published monographs in which the articles were signed with pseudonyms: EA was the pseudonym of Evola; Pietro Negri was that of Arturo Reghini; Luce was the pen name of G. Parise; Leo was used by the anthroposophist Colazza; and the appellation Abraxas was taken by the hermeticist Ercole Quadrelli.[†]

The Ur group published ten issues in 1927, two of which were double, and eight issues in 1928, two of which were double and one of which was triple. It was in October 1928 that the two directors of the journal, Reghini and Parise, departed.

Evola claimed that these two directors wanted to snatch away from him the publication of monographs by Ur so that they would be controlled by individuals who were keeping Freemasonry alive at a time when it was illegal in Italy. After this break, Evola alone remained responsible for the journal, which took the name *Krur*. Its last issue appeared in 1929.

In 1928 the Chacornac brothers offered to René Guénon the directorship of the journal *Le Voile d'Isis,* for which Grillot de Givry[15] was writing from time to time, though Guénon wanted to be just the editor.

Patrice Gentil contributed as well to this journal. Under the evocative pseudonym Mercuranus, he also wrote for *La Gnose,* published by the Librairie du Merveilleux, which was owned by Dujols and Thomas. He met René Guénon in 1908 at courses given at Papus's École Hermétique, in the Martinist Order, in the Église Gnostique, and ultimately in the

---

*Julius Evola wrote numerous books, among them *La Doctrine de l'Éveil*, his first book published in French (Paris: Éditions Adyar, 1956); in English, *The Doctrine of Awakening* (1948; reprint, Rochester, Vt.: Inner Traditions, 1996); and *Le Chemin de Cinabre* (Milan: Arché-Arkos, 1982). In addition to these titles, excellent monographs from the Ur group were published by Arché in Milan under the title *Introduction à la Magie* (in English, *Introduction to Magic,* Rochester, Vt.: Inner Traditions, 2001). They relate experiments and experiences conducted within the group and expound as well upon theories concerning different states of consciousness.

[†]Ercole Quadrelli was the author of an Italian translation of the alchemical treatise *Chymica Vannus*.

Ordre du Temple Rénové. He worked for the gas company as a meter reader, which allowed him to meet others who might have been, like himself, interested in Tradition. He was connected with the Kabbalist Paul Vulliaud and many others.

There were also ties between René Guénon and Madame Dina. Heiress to one of America's largest fortunes, Madame Dina was the wife of an alchemist whose work was just beginning to become known. Assan Farid Dina, of East Indian origin, was an electrical engineer, philosopher, and specialist in the religions and philosophies of India who gave lectures in Paris in 1911–12.

Assan Farid Dina transformed, modernized, and decorated the Château des Avenières at Cruseilles near Annecy (see fig. 2.1). In the chapel of this residence, gold-leaf mosaics representing the major arcana of the Tarot (see fig. 2.2) were discovered in 1967 by Bertrand Jacquet in the presence of several witnesses. It was the first time in the history of hermetic art that a chapel dedicated to the Tarot had been created using astonishing

*Fig. 2.1. The Château des Avenières, near Cruseilles (Haute-Savoie).*
*Property of A. F. Dina*

images from the cards. In 1978, in another chateau belonging to Dina, at Bar-sur-Seine, near Troyes, a temple to the Tarot (incorporating bas-reliefs representing the minor arcana) was discovered, as was his first alchemical book, *La Science Philosophique* (Philosophic Science), published in 1917 under the pseudonym A. M. A., and his second book, *La Destinée: La Mort et Ses Hypothèses* (Destiny, Death, and Their Hypotheses), published in 1927 under his real name just shortly before his passing.

Dina is said to be buried in Egypt, but in fact the mystery of his death and the location of his tomb has never been solved. The Dina Foundation[16] is soon to publish a book on his life and work as an adept who was a contemporary of Guénon and Fulcanelli.

After the death of her husband, Madame Dina founded the Véga Bookstore at 43 rue Madame, and took on René Guénon as director of her series "L'Anneau d'Or" (The Golden Ring), which she had created for him. She came close to embarking on a second marriage with him and lived with him for several months at Avenières.

René Guénon, accompanied by Madame Dina, left for Egypt on March 5, 1930, in an effort to find Sufi texts for the series. Because the sojourn there took longer than expected, however, Madame Dina had to return to Paris alone.

Upon her return, she met Ernest Britt at the home of Dr. Rouhier, the commercial director of Véga, and the two were married. Her new husband hated René Guénon and was the cause of the break between him and Madame Dina. She stopped sending Guénon money and turned over to Dr. Rouhier the management of the bookstore and its publishing house, Éditions Véga. This turn of events placed René Guénon in a difficult financial situation.

Ernest Britt, firm friend of Oswald Wirth, belonged to a group of occultists that also included Piobb (Pierre Vincenti). As for Alexandre Rouhier,* he too belonged to a secret society, called Le Grand Lunaire

---

*Alexandre Rouhier's book *De l'Architecture Naturelle* (Concerning Natural Architecture), which he principally authored with the participation of Marcel Nicaud, was published by Véga. He was also the author of *La Plante qui fait les yeux émerveillés—le peyolt* (The Plant That Fills the Eyes with Marvels—Peyote) published by Doin in 1927.

*Fig. 2.2. One of the mosaics in the chapel of the chateau, representing the seventeenth card of the Tarot deck, the Star.*

(The Great Lunary), which based its work on books by *René Schwaller de Lubicz,* Crowley, and Fulcanelli.

Robert Ambelain informs us about the participants in this strange assembly and mentions *Jules Boucher* and *Jean-Julien Champagne* (fig. 2.3), as well as *Gaston Sauvage,* who directed the Grand Lunaire's section on black and satanic magic. The baphomet served as their emblem. It is said that when Jules Boucher left the Grand Lunaire— with difficulty, it should be noted—he had to have himself exorcised at Lyons by the gnostic bishop Monseigneur Jean Bricaud. He was

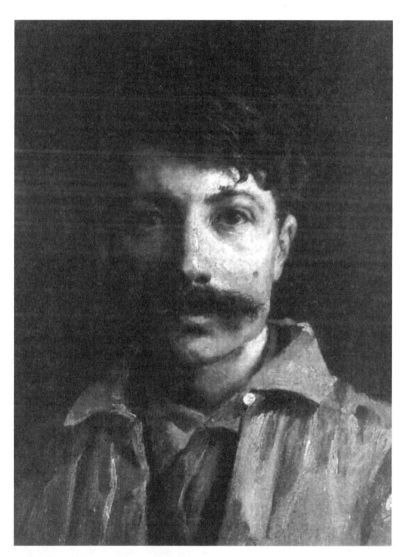

*Fig. 2.3. Self-portrait of Jean-Julien Champagne at the age of twenty-five. On the back of the painting is the date May 6, 1902, the number 136, and a red seal with the inscription "Julien Champagne, artist-painter, Paris."*

terrorized by the members of this society, especially by Gaston Sauvage. It should be mentioned that he had been subjected to the Ceremony of the Curse.

In Robert Amadou's *Feu du Soleil* (The Fire of the Sun), *Eugène Canseliet* gives Rouhier, Boucher, and Champagne as members of the Grand Lunaire. He claims that Champagne allowed himself to be dragged into a deplorable collaboration, and that Rouhier and Boucher "often went at night to the dolmen of Meudon, armed with their portable *occultum* from the Grand Lunaire."

*Part 2*

# MILIEU

Copiapite

Essential oil

Vinegar

Glass

Talc

Subacetate of copper

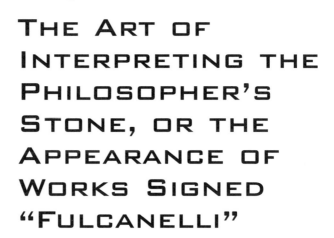

*3*

# THE ART OF INTERPRETING THE PHILOSOPHER'S STONE, OR THE APPEARANCE OF WORKS SIGNED "FULCANELLI"

We have just viewed a picture of the occultist ferment at the end of the nineteenth century and the beginning of the twentieth. In this we have been able to identify most of the players who participated in the creation of the most fabulous legend there has ever been: the myth of the adept Fulcanelli.

Let us now investigate in more detail this fascinating business and see how a few individuals, all connected by their membership in groups concerned with magic or spiritualism or in the Freemasonry movement, were able, owing to the publication of two books, to assist the resurgence of alchemy.

It is appropriate first to point out that for a long time—since the sixteenth century, in fact—Gothic architecture had been considered barbaric. This was true to such an extent that during the French Revolution, a decree was issued ordering the destruction of Notre Dame Cathedral in Paris. We owe the preservation of this marvelous edifice to the intelligence of one man: Charles-François Dupuy pointed out that the cathedral's sculptures contained teachings on science, art, and philosophy, and, in doing so, saved it from destruction.[1] In 1831, Victor Hugo published his novel *Notre-Dame-de-Paris*. In its composition he had drawn from material in alchemical works—but he allowed an odor of sulfur to emanate from his philosopher of hermetic science. It was thanks to this book, however, that public opinion was sensitized and that the architect Viollet-le-Duc was able to undertake restoration work on the building starting in 1845.

In his *Cours de Philosophie Hermétique* (Course in Hermetic Philosophy), François Cambriel presented this monument as an edifice with an alchemical character. Before him, Esprit Gobineau de Montluisant[2] had already addressed this question in his book in which he reveals the hermetic aspects of Notre Dame.

Nevertheless, it was not until 1926 that there appeared, to general indifference, a book with the title *Le Mystère des Cathédrales*. Signed "Fulcanelli," and with a press run of three hundred copies, it was published by Schémit at 45 rue Laffite in Paris. *Le Mystère des Cathédrales* was followed in 1930 by *Les Demeures Philosophales*, in one volume, similarly signed, and also published by Schémit.

Copiapite

Essential oil

Vinegar

Glass

Talc

Subacetate of copper

*4*

# PIERRE DUJOLS AND THE LIBRAIRIE DU MERVEILLEUX

On January 23, 1877, at 10:10 in the morning, when Jean-Julien Champagne was born at Levallois-Perret in the département of the Seine, his parents, both twenty-three years old, had no idea that their child would lead a life that was out of the ordinary, and that he would leave a mark on history. In fact, he was to be the actor in a prodigious adventure connected with humanity's most fabulous myth: that of the philosopher's stone.

Fifteen years earlier, at Saint-Illide in the Cantal region, on March 22, 1862, at 7:00 A.M., Pierre Dujols* was born. He belonged to one of the most illustrious families in France: the Valois. At that time his father was engaged in the trade of shoemaker, and his mother, Toinette Lapeyre, was not engaged in a profession. Pierre was the youngest of three children; in 1862 his father was forty and his mother forty-four. These two individuals—Champagne and Dujols— whose paths ought not to have crossed, sought out each other's company and formed a remarkable and complementary tandem. (See figs. 4.1 and 4.2 for copies of the birth certificates of Champagne and Dujols.)

---

*The natal charts of Dujols and Champagne are discussed in appendices H and I, respectively.

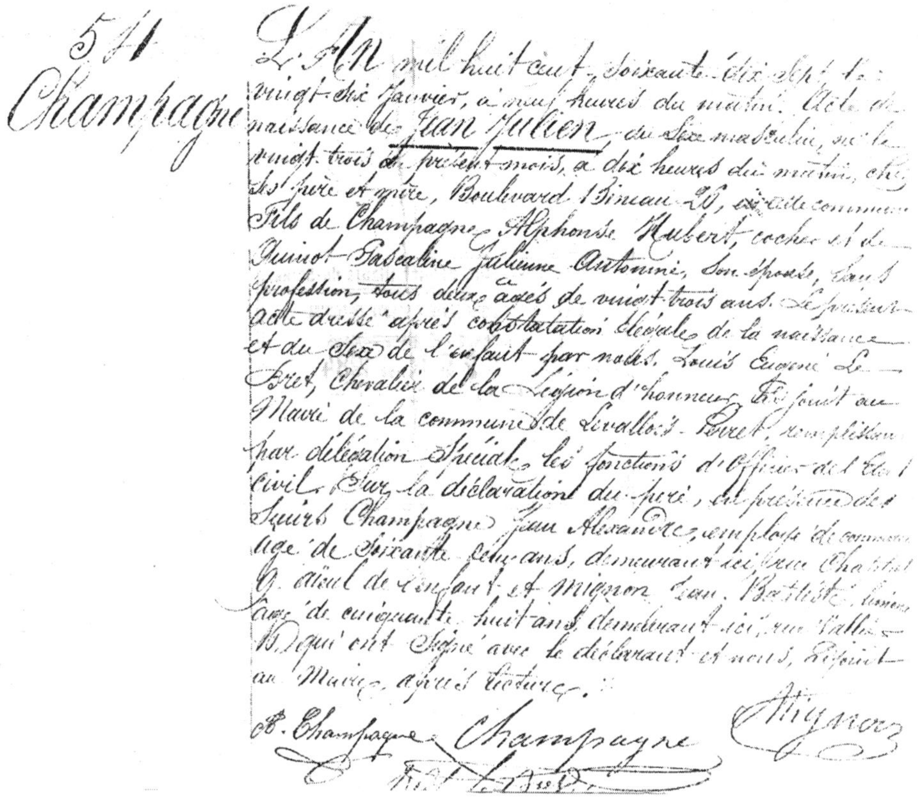

*Fig. 4.1. Jean-Julien Champagne's birth certificate*

With his mother's help, Jean-Julien Champagne, scarcely sixteen years of age and fascinated by the study of ancient alchemical texts, installed a laboratory in the family home at Villiers-le-Bel. There he devoted himself to his favorite pastime and acquired skills that would later be very useful for his experiments and would allow him to become a functioning alchemist of prime quality.

He continued to study passionately in Parisian libraries, where precious manuscripts are ferreted away.

At the same time, he registered at the École des Beaux-Arts in Paris. His registration card, number 5996, informs us of his progress as a student of the painter Léon Gérôme. From this period, an excellent painting has survived depicting the bishop of Bordeaux. There are also three of his

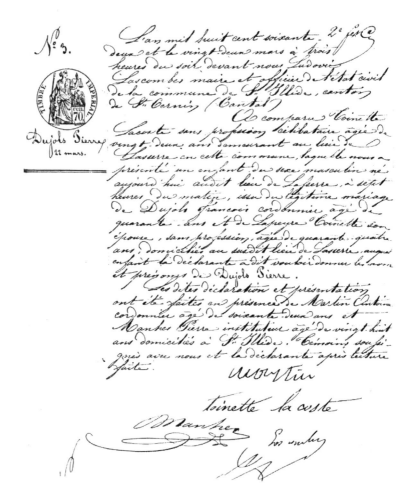

*Fig. 4.2. Extract from Pierre Dujols's birth certificate*

watercolors from 1895 (see fig. 4.3) and a photograph of a very beautiful miniature pendulum clock that he carved to represent a Gothic church, thereby demonstrating his early interest in the Middle Ages (see fig. 4.4). Other examples of his work are reproduced in figures 4.5 and 4.6.

In 1900 he graduated from the École Nationale et Spéciale des Beaux-Arts. He was twenty-three years old, an attractive man of medium build, 5 feet 7 inches tall, with a mustache. He had great success with the ladies, which continued all his life.

*Fig. 4.3. Watercolor by Champagne: "Beauvoir-Rivière," Soleil Couchant,
August 9, 1895*

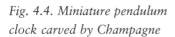

*Fig. 4.4. Miniature pendulum
clock carved by Champagne*

*Fig. 4.5. Drawings from the pen of Champagne, May 31, 1898*

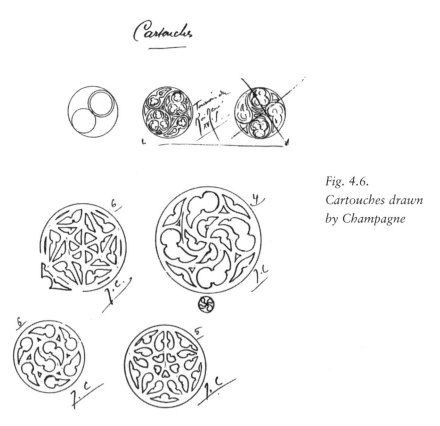

*Fig. 4.6.*
*Cartouches drawn*
*by Champagne*

The era was rife with possibilities. Numerous personalities gathered in specialized shops, attracted by the mutual desire of meeting and studying together.

One such place, the Librairie du Merveilleux (Bookstore of the Marvelous), founded by Chamuel, was located at 76 rue de Rennes in the 6th arrondissement of Paris. It was taken over by Pierre Dujols and Alexandre Thomas and moved to this location, becoming, during the years 1910–11, the gathering place of Hellenistic scholars and well-known Kabbalists. In his book *La Vie Simple de René Guénon* (The Simple Life of René Guénon), Paul Chacornac describes this place for us. On entering, the visitor passed a wrought-iron portico and then crossed a flagstone courtyard in front of the building; the bookstore occupied the second floor, within the staff quarters of the former Chemilly Hotel.[1]

In this setting ideas circulated concerning a famous language of signs, forgotten but not lost, called *la langue verte,* "the green tongue," or the language of the birds. The master of these quarters, Pierre Dujols, was a scholar of Greek literature and a staunch defender of the Hellenic language, which he insisted was the origin of the French language, and which allowed him, through the etymology of alchemical terms that it provided, to apply a particular calculation called the *hermetic cabala* to words and expressions and, by means of this device, to find a precise meaning that was helpful to laboratory work. He maintained a one-of-a-kind archive on occult sciences that his friend Jean-Julien Champagne later used. For the time being, his disciple in hermetic science, Faugeron* (at the time a traveling salesman living at 6 rue des Sabots), was responsible for updating this resource. This same Faugeron, along with Alexandre Thomas, belonged

---

*L. Faugeron was the laboratory helper of Pierre Dujols, who, being ill, could not work himself. After Dujols's death, Faugeron continued his research, sacrificing everything to buy charcoal and alchemical books. Some say he died of hunger, in total destitution, without having attained the realization of his efforts.

Contrary to what can be found in print, Pierre Dujols held that laboratory work was essential. He replied one day to his friend Paul Le Cour, who considered alchemy an inner discipline, "that he was completely wrong and that it was impossible to understand intellectual hermetic science without working on material substances, that hermetic terminology cannot be correlated with scientific terminology."

to René Guénon's Ordre du Temple Rénové. Thomas and Guénon, as well as Desjobert, the medium, were "excommunicated" from Martinism in 1909 by Papus and Téder. All three were also Freemasons. Pierre Dujols was passionate about alchemy and was very discreet. He left behind few traces to prove it, but it is said that he was keenly interested in this field. An article in *Charivari* entitled "l'Ère du Verseau" (The Age of Aquarius) provides an echo of this for us:*

---

*On February 23, 1925, Pierre Dujols wrote the following letter, which summarizes the file that had been passed on to him from Paul Le Cour concerning the famous Hiéron du Val d'Or:

Dear Sir and Friend:

I have begun the study of the two notebooks that you have passed on to me. We do learn something from them. Not only do the Adherents of Hiéron promote themselves as Templars and Knights of the Grail, but furthermore, they proclaim themselves "Apostles of the Final Times," those who were called for by the Virgin of la Salette in a secret connected with the Holy See. In addition, in this document, which has been published, the Apparition of la Salette implicates the clergy and "makes a pressing appeal to the Apostles of the Final Times, Those who know." Indeed, the promoters of this crusade boast of possessing Knowledge. There is some truth in these claims, but to what extent? . . .

The Adherents of Hiéron was also called the Société du Règne (Society of the Reign) or Société des Fastes (Society of the Glorious). This group was formed in 1875 by the Jesuit Drevon at Paray-le-Monial. His avowed purpose was to prove the reality of the reign of Christ and to prepare for his coming at the end of this cycle. Christianity was considered the flowering of the Primordial Tradition transmitted by the Atlanteans, according to Jacques d'Arès.

On this topic, also see Félix de Rosnay, *Le Hiéron du Val d'Or* (Paray-le-Monial, 1900).

Father Victor Drevon organized pilgrimages to Paray-le-Monial. In 1873, he met Baron Alexis de Sarachaga and, before his death in Rome in 1880, entrusted to him the task of founding the Société du Règne Social de Jésus-Christ (Society of the Reign of Jesus Christ in Society), the aim of which, in relation to the revelations of Sainte Marguerite-Marie, was "to offer to Jesus Christ the Host social reparations that he claimed himself at Paray in 1869."

Baron de Sarachaga, supporter of the claims to the French throne by Karl William Naundorff, devoted his efforts to the elaboration of Hiéron, a center from which would spread forth for forty years strange, millennial, hermetic doctrines. See Marie-France James, *Ésotérisme et Christianisme autour de René Guénon* (Esotericism and Christianity around René Guénon, Paris: Nouvelles Éditions Latines, 1981).

Not only do the adherents of Hiéron promote themselves as Templars and Knights of the Grail, but furthermore do they proclaim themselves as "Apostles of the Final Times," those who were called for by the Virgin of la Salette. . . ." These lines were written in 1925 by a Parisian bookstore owner named Pierre Dujols—strange man, very scholarly, and according to some, passionate about esotericism and alchemy.[2]

In his book *La Pierre Philosophale* (The Philosopher's Stone), in the chapter entitled "Quelques réflexions" (Some Thoughts), the engineer Georges Ranque provides information on Pierre Dujols and his connection with alchemy. He writes: "Based on their writings, we would think that Magophon and Auriger were familiar with the practice of the work. For me, who knew them well, I can state that they were acquainted with the theory, but the mystery of Mercury and bringing it to life remained for them unsolved all their lives. One of the last authors who would have succeeded is Cyliani, whose treatise appeared in 1832."[3]

Note that the pseudonym of Dujols is Magophon (Voice of the Mage) and that Georges Ranque does not include Fulcanelli as a possible adept.

Concerning the name Cyliani, Eugène Canseliet agrees with attributing its authorship to Pierre Dujols. In *Feu du Soleil* (Fire of the Sun), he declares to Robert Amadou: "I add then Cyliani. What a pseudonym! It's Pierre Dujols who gave him this name." In *L'Alchimie expliquée sur ses textes classiques* (Alchemy Explained according to Its Classic Texts), Eugène Canseliet points out that he *does not know* who filled out the name following the first syllable *Ci* . . . in Cyliani, a name that is based on the Silenus who converses with Midas.[4]

As for the works of Fulcanelli, which remain invaluable, they inform us about the etymology of this term: "Cyliani is the equivalent of Cyllenius, from Mount Cyllene, the mountain where Mercury [Hermes] was born and which gave this Cyllenian god his name."[5]

The perceptive reader will note a contradiction: *Hermès Dévoilé*

(Hermes Unveiled), the publication attributed to Cyliani, appeared in 1832. Upon republication of the book by Chacornac in 1915, Pierre Dujols, who was born in 1862, could well have filled out the *Ci . . .* that stood for the author's name. Yet in 1834, two years after the appearance of *Hermès Dévoilé,* we find published in Paris the *Nouveau Recueil d'Ouvrages Anonymes et Pseudonymes* (New Collection of Anonymous and Pseudonymous Works) by a Mr. de Manne. On page 157, under work numbered 727, the pseudonym Cyliani appears for the first time.[6]

Pierre Dujols, then, could have reused this name but he could not have originated it, for in 1834 he had not yet been born.

Fortunately, he did leave us a single book written under the pseudonym Magophon, entitled *Mutus Liber* (The Mute Book),[7] preceded by an *hypotypose.** In it he develops very interesting ideas, which we shall find later in works attributed to Fulcanelli and which concern Kermes, celestial agriculture, the composition of an egg, the oak barrel, photography and salts, nostoc,[†] the reference to Thomas Corneille, and so on.

In his youth, Pierre Dujols accompanied his parents when they left the Cantal region and moved to Marseilles. This was how he came to be an attentive student of the Jesuits of Aix-en-Provence, where he received a classical education. Having worked as a journalist in Marseilles and in Toulouse, he finally decided to live in Paris, at 47 rue Denfert-Rochereau (nowadays, rue Henri Barbusse). In Paris he organized a salon and hosted dinner parties. His soirées were highly regarded, for, in addition to his far-reaching knowledge, he was imbued with mystery concerning his ancestry. His brother Antoine, seventeen years his senior, had written a small pamphlet[8] of fifty-eight pages that appeared in Marseilles in 1879 and gave rise to controversy in the local press (the title page is reproduced in figure 4.8, page 37).

---

*[In English, a *hypotyposis,* which *Webster's Third* defines as a "vivid, picturesque description." —Ed.]

†[*Nostoc* is a kind of freshwater blue-green alga. —Ed.]

In this work studded with Latin quotations, Antoine Dujols demonstrates the dynastic legitimacy of his family.* He presents evidence to prove that the last member of the Valois line, the fourth son of Catherine de Medici and Henri II, did not die without leaving an heir. François de Valois, duke of Anjou and Alençon, married Jeanne Adélaïde, duchess of Médine Coeli, on April 12, 1575. From this marriage there arose a long line of male children, the last representative of which is Antoine Dujols de Valois, brother of Pierre, postman at Saint-Chamas, near Aix-en-Provence. Antoine Dujols de Valois was born on August 24, 1845, at Saint-Illide in the Cantal region (see fig. 4.9, page 38). In 1888, he lived in Marseilles at 43 boulevard du Nord, and in 1889 he ran in the legislative elections but was not elected. On July 12, 1892, he died at Salon in Provence at the age of forty-six.

---

*On pages 218–19 of his book *Du Roy perdu à Louis XVII* (From the Lost King to Louis XVII, Paris: Julliard, 1967), a historical psychoanalysis of a national myth, Éric Muraise quotes from the book by Antoine Dujols de Valois:

> François de Valois, duke of Alençon and brother of the former duke, also would have married in a foreign country. In 1575, he married Jeanne de Medina Coeli in Spain. Under Louis XV, the descendants of this marriage are to be found in France in the person of Charles-Louis de Valois. He died at the Bastille and his wife became insane. Her son was then adopted by a workman named Guillaume Dujol. In 1885, we find a Dujol bringing to the court of Aurillac a request for a correction of his civil status in order to be recognized as Henri-Charles-Louis d'Usson, d'Auvergne, d'Alençon, prince of Valois. It doesn't seem that the court acted upon this strange request, yet there are still people using the name Dujol. In the regions of Lyons and Auvergne before the last war, we found a "royal league" devoted to the cause of Monseigneur Henri de Valois, which was confused with the cause of a Henri Dujol.
>
> In admitting the reality of the Polish marriage and the Spanish marriage of our two Valois, we must be clear that their civil and monarchic values were not the same. If they were legitimate, they were definitely not authorized, which would be enough to exclude their offspring from royal succession.

*Author's note:* The reference to the "Polish marriage" relates to the brother of François de Valois, Henri III, who would have entered into two marriages—one in 1573 with a Polish woman and the other with Louise de Vaudémont.

*Fig. 4.7. Antoine Dujols de Valois (left), and Pierre Dujols de Valois as a young man*

His death was recorded among the obituaries in the July 17, 1892, issue of the paper *L'Avant-Garde de Provence*, an establishment-oriented, Catholic literary weekly. It reads as follows:

> Mr. de Valois, whom we knew and respected, has just died, imbued with feelings of the most profound faith, in the town of Salon, after a long and painful illness. The tuberculosis patients to whom he had devoted a part of his life completely selflessly will have lost in him not only a friend but a *healer*. Having witnessed several recoveries, which we believed to be resurrections, our conscience impels us to state this fact publicly. We extend to his brother and his mother our most sincere condolences.

So he was a thaumaturgist.*

---

*[*Webster's Third* defines *thaumaturgist* as "a performer of miracles, especially a magician." —*Ed.*]

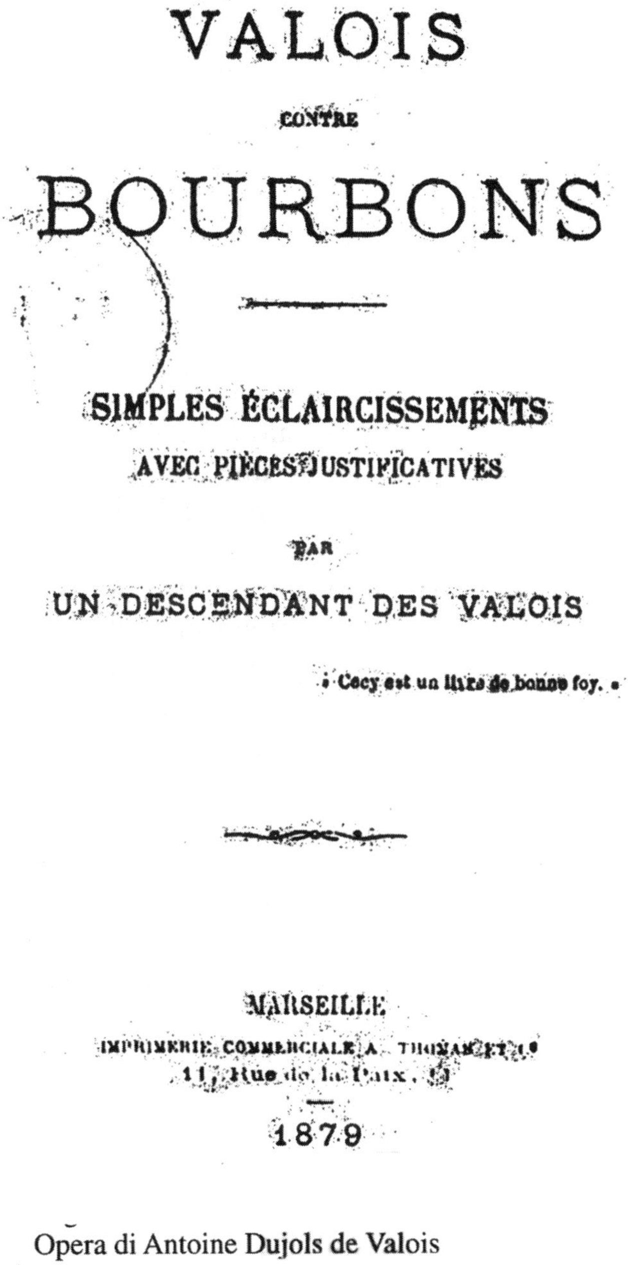

# VALOIS

### contre

# BOURBONS

---

## SIMPLES ÉCLAIRCISSEMENTS

### AVEC PIÈCES JUSTIFICATIVES

#### PAR

## UN DESCENDANT DES VALOIS

« Cecy est un livre de bonne foy. »

## MARSEILLE

IMPRIMERIE COMMERCIALE A. THOMAS ET Cⁱᵉ
11, Rue de la Paix, 9

### 1879

Opera di Antoine Dujols de Valois

*Fig. 4.8. Title page of the book written by Antoine Dujols de Valois*

MAIRIE DE
SAINT-ILLIDE
(CANTAL)

RÉPUBLIQUE FRANÇAISE

# EXTRAIT D'ACTE DE NAISSANCE

ÉTAT CIVIL

Registre Naissance

Année 1845

Acte N° 36.

Le (1) Vingt quatre août mil huit cent quarante cinq à trois heure est né en notre commune: (2)

DUGEOLS Antoine

du sexe masculin

de (3) françois DUGEOLS Cordonnier

et de (3) antoinette LAPEYRE, son épouse, demeurants audit lieu de Lasserre St Illide

Mentions marginales (4)

Pour extrait conforme :

Le 30 OCT. 1987

Signature,

SEDI - 30700 UZES - Modèle 301040

(1) Quantième en chiffres, mais mois en lettres.
(2) Prénoms et nom patronymique.
(3) Prénoms, nom, lieu et date de naissance, profession et domicile des parents et indication de la qualité d'époux des père et mère. Toutefois, ces indications ne doivent figurer que sur les extraits destinés aux héritiers, aux administrations publiques ou aux personnes susceptibles d'obtenir, aux termes de l'article 57 du Code Civil, la copie intégrale de l'acte de naissance. Elles ne doivent pas figurer dans l'extrait délivré à tout requérant.
(4) Dans l'extrait délivré à tout requérant, cette rubrique ne doit être remplie qu'en ce qui concerne le mariage.

*Fig. 4.9. Extract from Antoine Dujols's birth certificate*

In addition to his book *Valois contre Bourbons* (The Conflict between the Valois and the Bourbons), he wrote a curious little pamphlet of twenty-six pages on the regeneration of grapevines. He published it himself under the name A. de Valois, and affixed his signature to the last page.

The family of Pierre Dujols tells anecdotally that his brother, Antoine, called on the Orléans family in Paris in order to show them important proofs in his possession concerning his genealogy, and that the family consented to see him. Later, in the town of Salon, where Antoine lived, burglars broke into the quarters he shared with his mother on the rue d'Avignon, attacked them both, and stole these documents as well as the ring that he owned.

The Valois family line continued no further, for Antoine had no offspring and his brother, Pierre, had no sons and two daughters—Yvonne, born in 1888, and Marguerite, born in 1900. One of them was a reader for the duchess of Portland. Pierre's wife, whose maiden name was Charton, was a woman of rare beauty who, despite her youth, had very long white hair. A native of Hennebont, in Brittany, she married Pierre Dujols in 1887 when she was only nineteen and he was twenty-five.*

Madame Dujols was gifted with a remarkable clairvoyance; she performed card readings and palmistry and very often had premonitory dreams.

Regarding Hennebont, we should recall the story of the ring that Fulcanelli owned and which, according to Mr. Canseliet, originated with the abbé of a Cistercian monastery that in the twelfth century was a commandery of the Knights Templar of Hennebont.

The salon of the Dujols, in the 5th arrondissement of Paris, was frequented by those involved in the world of esotericism. Among

---

*Madame Dujols was born in the département of Morbihan on February 2, 1868, at 2:00 A.M. on the rue Neuve in Hennebont. She was the daughter of Nicolas Joseph Charton, fifty-three (civil servant in charge of road maintenance), and Caroline Perrine Leroux, thirty-five (no profession). She died in Paris in the 7th arrondissement on October 8, 1954. Her sister Anna became a nun with the Sisters of Clare at Millhill near London, using the name Sister Clothilde.

them was the well-known Kabbalist, and old friend of Pierre Dujols, Paul Vulliaud, who had a considerable interest in the hermetic cabala. Oswald Wirth as well as René Guénon also attended regularly and participated in the exchange of ideas.

We should recall that in 1905, René Guénon, along with a few young people from Martinism (Thomas and Faugeron among them), created the famous Ordre du Temple Rénové. The woman who was the concierge at 47 rue Denfert-Rochereau reported later that Pierre Dujols himself directed the rituals of the order. The husband of the concierge also participated in the séances. He was a close friend of Dujols and, oddly, passed away one day after he did.

The Ordre du Temple Rénové was disbanded in 1911. This was also the year that Pierre Dujols fell seriously ill with the osteoarthritis from which he died on April 19, 1926, at the age of sixty-four. It was difficult for him to move around, and in 1921, five years before his death, he became bedridden. Eugène Canseliet saw him in this state, "lying on his sickbed with his folded knees serving as his desk."

He nevertheless continued to study alchemy, and in 1914 he published *Mutus Liber* with an *hypotypose*. This same year his associate Thomas was killed in the war. This was also a loss for Jean-Julien Champagne, who was Thomas's faithful friend.

Pierre Dujols was very connected to esoteric circles. A letter that he wrote to Papus, addressed "Dear Master," conveys the esteem with which he regarded Dr. Encausse (see fig. 4.11). This missive is undated but must nevertheless have been written between 1912, the date of the closing of the Librairie du Merveilleux, and 1915–16, for Papus died in 1916.*

Although Dujols's associates included many who were involved in Freemasonry, nowhere have we found evidence of his belonging to this movement, nor, furthermore, to Martinism. But the striking involvement in his life of personalities from these two movements no doubt allowed

---

*The brother of Alexandre-Albéric Thomas (known as Marnès), whose name was Abel Thomas, grand master of the Order of Memphis-Misraïm, continued to oppose the regular admission of Papus to Freemasonry. He notes this in an article that appeared in the January 1907 issue of the journal *Acacia*.

Fig. 4.10. Pierre
Dujols de Valois as
an older man

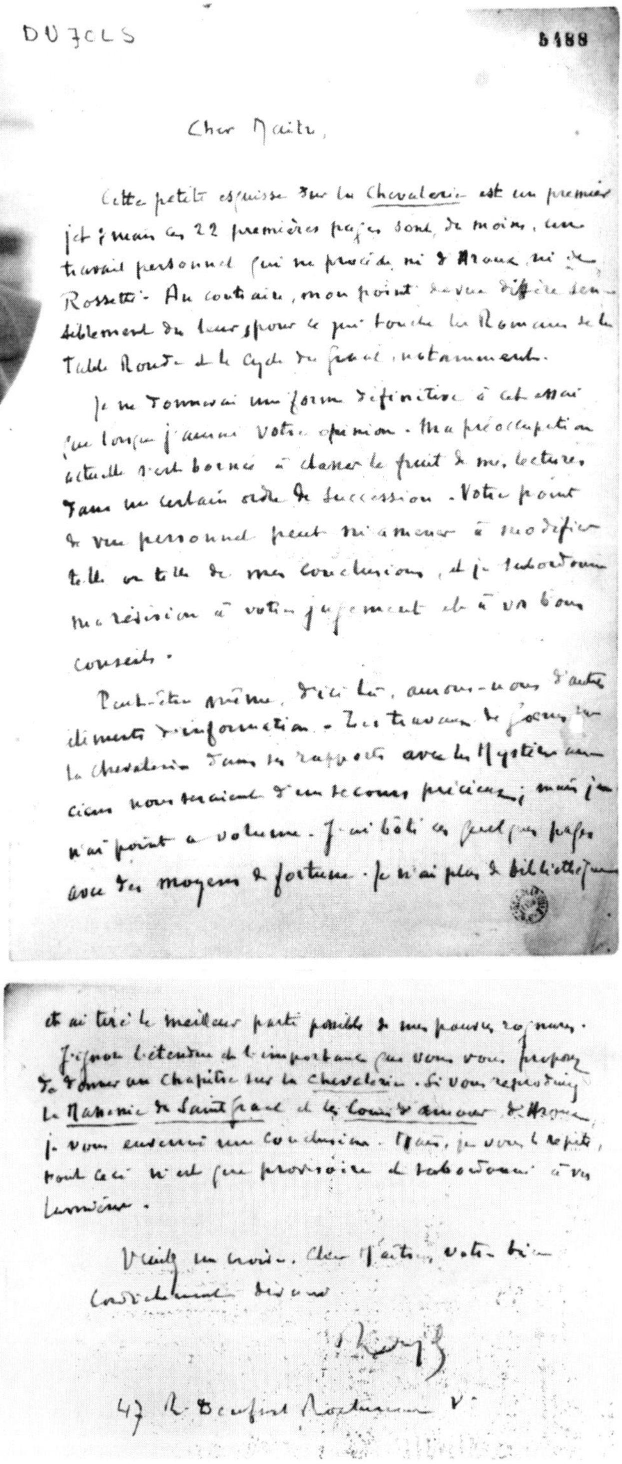

Fig. 4.11. Letter
from Pierre Dujols
to Papus

him to have heard of, or even to have known, the scholarly philologist and archaeologist Grasset d'Orcet. Dujols, who died in 1926, and d'Orcet, who died in 1900, could have visited each other or even written to each other, maintaining a correspondence much like that of Engineering Commander Levet[9] and Grasset d'Orcet. Both Levet and d'Orcet were fascinated by cryptography and exchanged more than three hundred letters. Papus, an acquaintance of Pierre Dujols's, received a letter from Commander Levet, a Freemason of the Grand Orient Lodge, that seems to prove the connection among these different individuals (fig. 4.12). Furthermore, in 1911

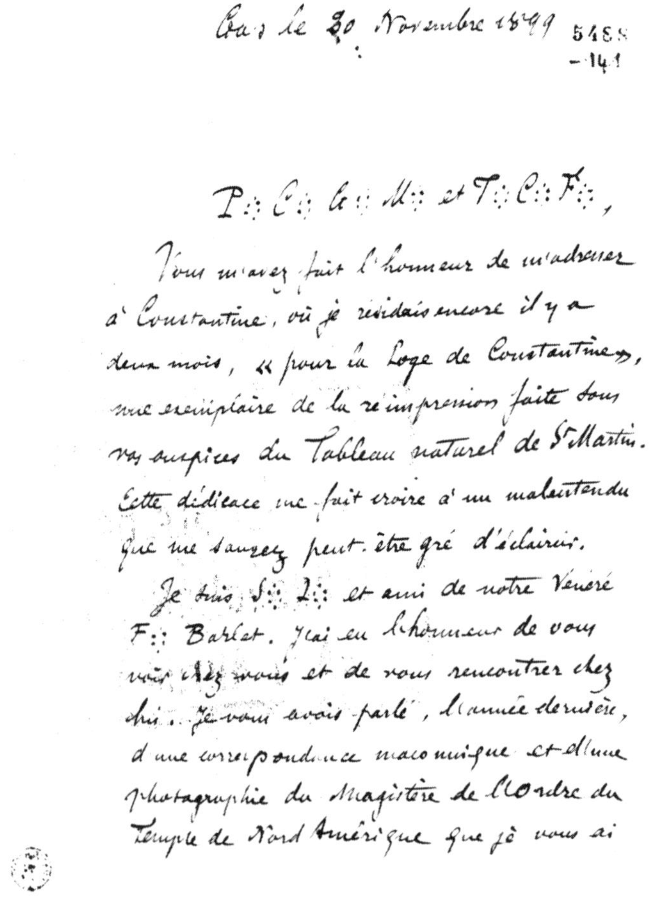

Bar, le 30 Novembre 1899 5488 -141

P∴ C∴ le∴ M∴ et T∴ C∴ F∴,

Vous m'avez fait l'honneur de m'adresser à Constantine, où je résidais encore il y a deux mois, « pour la Loge de Constantine », un exemplaire de la réimpression faite sous vos auspices du Tableau naturel de St Martin. Cette dédicace me fait croire à un malentendu que vous saurez peut-être gré d'éclaircir.

Je suis S∴ I∴ et ami de notre Vénéré F∴ Barlet. J'ai eu l'honneur de vous voir chez vous et de vous rencontrer chez lui. Je vous avais parlé, l'année dernière, d'une correspondance maçonnique et d'une photographie du Magistère de l'Ordre du Temple de Nord Amérique que je vous ai

*Fig. 4.12. Letter from Commander Levet to Papus. Levet had frequent correspondence with Grasset d'Orcet.*

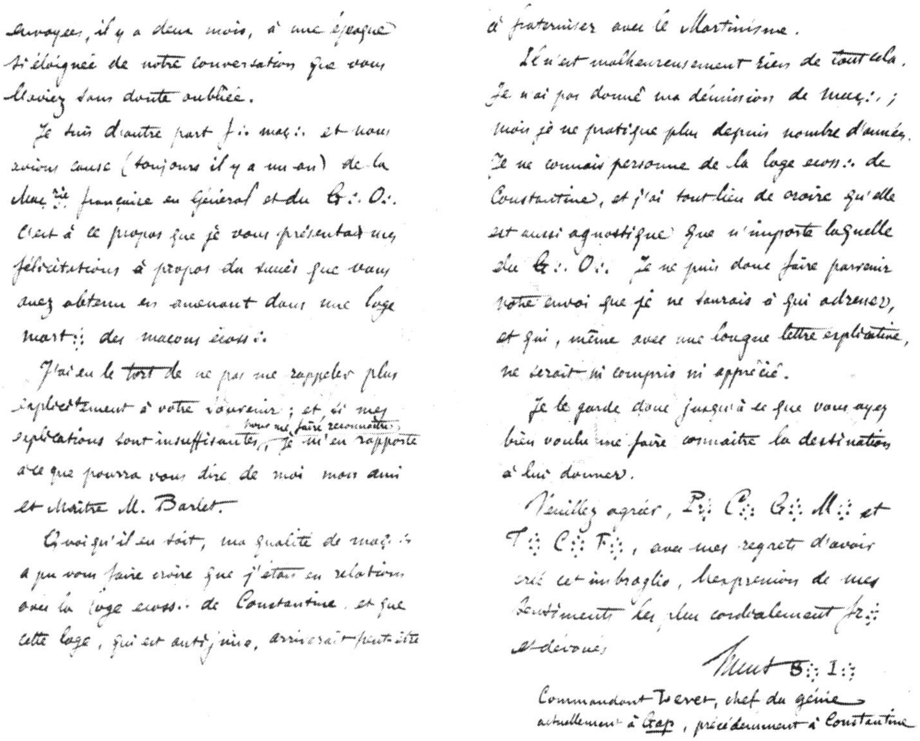

envoyées, il y a deux mois, à une époque si éloignée de notre conversation que vous l'aviez sans doute oubliée.

Je suis d'autre part f∴ maç∴ et nous avions causé (toujours il y a un an) de la Maç∴ française en Général et du G∴ O∴. C'est à ce propos que je vous présentai mes félicitations à propos du succès que vous avez obtenu en amenant dans une loge mart∴ des maçons écoss∴.

J'ai eu le tort de ne pas me rappeler plus explicitement à votre souvenir ; et, si mes explications sont insuffisantes, pour me faire reconnaître, je m'en rapporte à ce que pourra vous dire de moi mon ami et Maître M. Barlet.

Quoiqu'il en soit, ma qualité de maç∴ a pu vous faire croire que j'étais en relation avec la loge écoss∴ de Constantine, et que cette loge, qui est antijuive, arriverait peut-être à fraterniser avec le Martinisme.

Il n'est malheureusement rien de tout cela. Je n'ai pas donné ma démission de maç∴ ; mais je ne pratique plus depuis nombre d'années. Je ne connais personne de la loge écoss∴ de Constantine, et j'ai tout lieu de croire qu'elle est aussi agnostique que n'importe laquelle du G∴ O∴. Je ne puis donc faire parvenir votre envoi que je ne saurais à qui adresser, et qui, même avec une longue lettre explicative, ne serait ni compris ni apprécié.

Je le garde donc jusqu'à ce que vous ayez bien voulu me faire connaître la destination à lui donner.

Veuillez agréer, P∴ C∴ G∴ M∴ et T∴ C∴ F∴, avec mes regrets d'avoir créé cet imbroglio, l'expression de mes sentiments les plus cordialement fr∴ et dévoués

[illegible] B∴ I∴

Commandant Tever, chef du génie
actuellement à Gap, précédemment à Constantine

a translation of the English *The Mystical Traditions* by the theosophist Isabel Cooper-Oakley, which quotes Grasset d'Orcet, appeared in Paris under the title *Traditions mystiques.*

Grasset d'Orcet was born at Aurillac in the Cantal region not far from Saint-Illide, home territory of the Dujols de Valois family and birthplace of Pierre Dujols. Along with others, he believed in strange reading techniques, which he had discovered in two stages. Applicable to texts as important as those of Rabelais, these techniques allowed readers to discover that underlying an apparently commonplace text is a second layer of meaning transmitting a teaching or providing political revelations. His work appeared in the *Revue Britannique,* a journal published between 1825 and 1901 and founded by Louis-Sébastien Saulnier with the aim of promulgating literary and scientific news from England.

Fulcanelli quotes Grasset d'Orcet in *Le Mystère des Cathédrales,* in the chapter on the Cyclic Cross of Hendaye concerning Grasset d'Orcet's analysis of the *Songe de Poliphile,*[10] which first appeared in an article in the *Revue.* Applying cryptographic keys to this work, Grasset d'Orcet claims that "[t]he *Dream of Poliphilus* is none other than a Masonic grimoire—that is, an encoded text applied to architecture, no different from more modern treatises of this kind except for the incomparable richness and nobility of its structures."

Grasset d'Orcet demonstrated an amazing erudition and a nearly exclusive interest in the Greek language.*

Another personality aroused the curiosity of the little group forming around the Dujols family. Fulcanelli speaks of this in his book *Les Demeures Philosophales,* at the beginning of the chapter on the hermetic cabala.

In the year 1843, those conscripts assigned to the 46th Infantry Regiment garrisoned at Paris† could meet each week with a very uncommon professor by proceeding across the courtyard of the

---

*The following biography of Grasset d'Orcet is drawn from *Matériaux cryptographiques,* vol. 1, collected and arranged by Bernard Allieu and A. Barthélémy.

Born on June 6, 1828, at Aurillac in the Cantal region, d'Orcet engaged in the study of classics at Clermont-Ferrand, then at Juilly (département Seine-et-Marne) and graduated in law in Paris, where he was a regular at the workshop of a sculptor from whom he acquired a good understanding of art. Upon the death of his father, he undertook a study tour of the Mediterranean, at the end of which he settled in Cyprus. There he studied the remnants of cryptographic systems of ancient Greece. A change in his fortunes interrupted his archaeological research and obliged him to return to France, where he collaborated on various publications. In December 1873, the *Revue Britannique* accepted an initial article from him, which was the beginning of an abundant and varied series. Over a period of twenty-seven years, he produced 160 articles on a diverse range of topics, some reaching, in the case of the longest ones, two hundred pages. Removing himself from the world, d'Orcet devoted his life to labors that were truly monastic. He died at Cusset (département Allier) on December 2, 1900.

†The 46th Infantry Regiment was garrisoned not in Paris but in Caen—according to the yearbook of the army for the year 1843 and according to *L'Historique du 46ᵉ Régiment d'Infanterie* by Chaperon, in the archives at Vincennes.

Louis-Philippe barracks. . . . In the evening he taught the history of France to the soldiers who wanted to attend, requiring a modest fee and using a method that he claimed had been known in the most remote antiquity. In reality, this course that was so attractive for those who attended was based on traditional phonetic cabala.

This unique professor described by Fulcanelli—Allévy, the only teacher of this method—is the author of a little pamphlet, *L'Histoire de France, Allévysée*. (He published the pamphlet himself; see figure 4.13 for the title page.) The examples chosen by the alchemist can be found in this book, with minor variations.

The mnemonic technique employed by this method and elaborated on by the congenial Allévy is based on rebus and wordplay (see fig. 4.14).

According to letters of recommendation and the congratulations that were addressed to him by the colonels (see fig. 4.15), it seems clear that his method was appreciated and that it gave excellent results.

Here is an example:

Clovis I, dit Le Grand ("Clovis I called the Great")
Un enfant est attaché sur une chaise par un grand clou à vis ("A child is attached to a chair by a great nail with screw thread")

The structure can then be read as follows:

Grand clou-vis, Clovis, le grand ("Great nail-screw, Clovis, the Great")

Fulcanelli has Clovis ascending the throne in 466; Allévy, who is right, in 481.

Allévy was also the inventor of a perpetual dial mechanism (bought by King Léopold) showing days of the week and working for all calendar years between 1600 and 3099, as well as an "Allévy conjugator," which reduced all French verbs to a single conjugation.

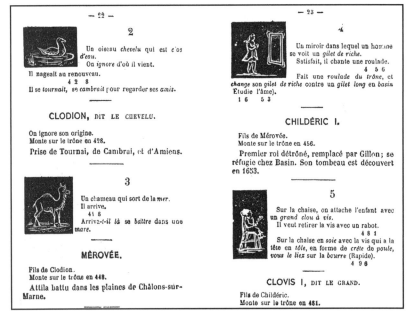

*Fig. 4.13. The book by Allévy (pictured at left) on the history of France taught according to his method*

*Fig. 4.14. Example of the Allévy method given by Fulcanelli*

— 8 —

MINISTÈRE
DE L'INTÉRIEUR.
INSTRUCTION
PUBLIQUE.
N° 3790.
Litt. A.

Bruxelles, le 4 avril 1833.

L'Administrateur général de
l'instruction publique,
A M. Allevy, chef d'institution,
rue des Arts, à Saint-Joos-ten-Noode.

Monsieur,

Le ministre de l'intérieur, à qui j'ai communiqué, ainsi que je vous l'ai fait savoir par ma lettre du 21 mars dernier, n° de la présente, le rapport favorable que j'ai reçu de M. l'Inspecteur Dewez, au sujet de votre établissement, vient de m'informer qu'il approuvait mes conclusions d'après lesquelles vous pouvez être envisagé comme *digne de la protection royale;* il observe toutefois que vous devez préalablement faire connaître de quelle manière vous désirez que cette protection se manifeste. Veuillez, en conséquence, m'adresser une demande spéciale et motivée à ce sujet, et je m'empresserai de la mettre sous les yeux du ministre.

Agréez, Monsieur, l'assurance de ma parfaite considération. LESBROUSSART.

M. Allevy a enseigné sa méthode pour l'histoire et la géographie, dans l'armée française, aux 1er, 4e, 21e, 25e, 34e, 35e, 37e, 40e, 46e, 48e, 54e, 58, 61e, 72e et 75e régiments d'infanterie de ligne; ensuite au 1er, 9e, 11e, 14e, 24e et 25e régiments d'infanterie légère; au 4e lanciers ; au 9e dragons et à la garde municipale.

Dans les inspections générales et dans toutes les circonstances où ils ont vu les élèves, les maréchaux de France, Magnan et Castellane, et les généraux de division et de brigade Schramm, Aulas de Courtigis, Taillandier, Delabordes, Aupick, Fabvier, Garraube Prévost, Sainte-Aldégonde, Rapatel, Boyer, Tholozé, Rumigny et Cubières, etc., ont continuellement approuvé et félicité l'inventeur sur ses succès.

Les certificats qui suivent, émanant des colonels

— 9 —

sous les yeux desquels les leçons ont été données, sont la plus sûre garantie de la rapidité et de la franchise des résultats.

Le colonel du 1er régiment d'infanterie de ligne soussigné, certifie que M. Allevy, professeur du levier intellectuel, a démontré l'histoire de France dans le régiment, et que sa méthode de Mnémonique a produit pour l'instruction de ses élèves les résultats les plus satisfaisants.
Paris, le 20 février 1846.

Le colonel PATÉ, présentement général de division, commandant la division d'Alger.

Le colonel du 51e de ligne, certifie que les leçons d'histoire de France, données aux sous-officiers et soldats du régiment, par M. Allevy, d'après sa méthode Mnémotechnique, ont produit d'excellents résultats.
Paris, le 16 mars 1846.

Le colonel baron MEYNARD.

Je soussigné, certifie que M. Allevy a démontré l'histoire de France aux sous-officiers de mon régiment, et que sa méthode Mnémonique a produit les résultats les plus satisfaisants.
Paris, le 9 avril 1846.

Le général de brigade, A. FRANÇOIS,
ex-colonel du 11e léger.

Le colonel soussigné, certifie que M. Allevy a fait dans le régiment, sous mes ordres, un cours d'histoire, par une méthode de son invention, dite le Levier intellectuel Allevy, qui a réussi en peu de temps et de la manière la plus satisfaisante. Les enfants mêmes ont appris par ce moyen l'histoire de France qu'ils possèdent parfaitement. Le colonel se plaît à reconnaître que M. Allevy a apporté dans son cours toute l'intelligence et tous les soins désirables, et qu'il a obtenu des ré-

1.

*Fig. 4.15. Various testimonials about the effectiveness of the Allévy method*

Pierre Dujols was a lover of music, which he had studied with the Jesuits at Aix-en-Provence. He was a chorister and had even written a book on music.

The famous singer Emma Calvé was very much in evidence at the salon and in the home of Mr. and Mrs. Dujols. She had a strong interest in esoteric science and was a regular at the bookstore of Edmond Bailly, L'Art Indépendant, where she met Debussy, Satie, and many others.

Born on August 15, 1858, at Decazeville, she was taken on by the Théâtre de la Monnaie, in Brussels, which proved to be the beginning of a splendid career. Her real name was Calvet, but her teacher Puget advised her to remove the *t* from her name for her life in the theater.

Contrary to what many authors have claimed, the lyric singer was not related to the clairvoyant from la Salette, Mélanie Calvat, whose name was really Calvat dit Mathieu.

Her lover was the famous Jules Bois, who was very involved in magic, and their relationship was well known. Bois, who was a handsome man from Marseilles, had been initiated into Lodge Number 7, AHATOR, of the Hermetic Order of the Golden Dawn. He wrote *Petites Religions de Paris* (Small Religions of Paris) in 1894, *Satanisme et la Magie* (Satanism and Magic) in 1895, and *Le Monde invisible* (The Invisible World) in 1902. He was also editor of the journal *Étoile,* produced by the bookstore L'Art Indépendant, where he no doubt met Emma Calvé. For her part, she bought a building called Cabrières, a small fortress that could have housed the mysterious kabbalistic work owned by Nicolas Flamel[11]—the book of Abraham known by the name *Aschmezareph*. This title was part of a larger work, the second segment of which was entitled *La Sagesse Divine* (Divine Wisdom). It was owned, it seems, by Stanislas de Guaita.

The name Emma Calvé is also known to us through her connection with Abbé Saunière, whose fame relates to the strange affair of Rennes-le-Château. This abbé, who was at least a little peculiar, had apparently discovered documents in the crypt of his church and had come to Paris in the hope of finding a knowledgable person who could help decipher them—whom he did meet at the church of Saint-Sulpice. Upon his return, in his own parish, he discovered (completely unexpectedly) a treasure trove as well as documents that proved the survival of a Merovingian family line. There exists extensive literature as well as a television film on this topic.

Abbé Saunière's associate Abbé Boudet, curé at Rennes-les-Bains, a village near his own, was an even more enigmatic figure. Abbé Boudet produced a work entitled *La Véritable Langue Celtique* (The Real Celtic Language)*—very scholarly and full of strange things—that

---

*Abbé H. Boudet, *La Vraie Langue Celtique et le Cromleck de Rennes-les-Bains* (Paris: Belfond, 1978), privately printed by the abbé in 1880 in an edition of three hundred copies. With his disciple Eugène Canseliet, Fulcanelli traveled to Limoux, near Rennes-les-Bains. There a cathedral can be found, Notre-Dame-de-Marceille, that houses a very beautiful Black Virgin. We should note that as a correction to the accepted history, Saint-Vincent-de-Paul stayed at Limoux, near Notre-Dame-de-Marceille, and not at Marseilles.

would have been not at all uninteresting to our friends at the Librairie du Merveilleux. In it he shows by means of the phonetic cabala that the single language that was spoken before Babel was modern English preserved by the Tectosages.[†]

Thus he gave a very instructive explanation of Genesis. Here is an example of his method:

Moïse (Moses; pronounced *moe-EEZ* in French)
To mow *(moe)*—that is, harvest
To ease *(eez)*—that is, deliver, release.

Moses worked in the fields and had been adopted by Pharaoh's daughter and thus delivered from his labors. This contradicts the official version, which holds that Moses was found in a basket floating on the water.

---

[†][An ancient Celtic tribe of France. —*Ed.*]

*Part 3*

# FULCANELLI
# UNVEILED

Copiapite

Essential oil

Vinegar

Glass

Talc

# 5

# JEAN-JULIEN CHAMPAGNE AND RENÉ SCHWALLER DE LUBICZ

In 1910, the young René Schwaller, then twenty-three, arrived in Paris. In the years prior to the war, he studied painting with Matisse and, very attracted to metaphysics, made contact with the Theosophical Society, which was then at its height. This association brought him into contact with numerous occultists and ardent spiritualists. He was also a regular at the Librairie du Merveilleux, where he was immediately fascinated by this group's interest in the phonetic cabala.

As an artist, he also frequented the home of Edmond Bailly, owner of L'Art Indépendant bookstore on the rue de la Chaussée-d'Antin, where a theatrical and artistic crowd regularly gathered.

It is this bookstore owned by Bailly that also published his first book, a study of numbers, a subject that fascinated him.[1]

In his free time he relaxed at the Closerie-des-Lilas café in Montparnasse. One day in 1913, a meeting took place there that would be significant for the circle of Jean-Julien Champagne and for the reemergence of alchemy as we now know it.

Subacetate of copper

The painter Jean-Julien Champagne, who had been the pupil of Léon Gérôme, was also a regular at this famous Parisian haunt. From 1907 on, he was connected to the de Lesseps family, who lived in a superb mansion on the avenue Montaigne in Paris. He gained entry to this wealthy milieu through the family chauffeur.

The sons of Ferdinand-Marie de Lesseps,* especially Bertrand and Ferdinand-Jules, were interested in, and in fact fascinated by, the science of Hermes. They suggested that Jean-Julien Champagne take up residence in the laboratory that Ferdinand owned on the rue Vernier, in the 17th arrondissement. It consisted of a two-room suite with a view of Mont Valérien. Champagne moved in and was therefore able to work on the development of the Great Work. He had as a disciple a man named Max Roset, and his material existence was ensured by the de Lesseps family, who employed him as an industrial designer.

It is in these quarters that Champagne engaged in the design of a propeller that later became the propulsion device on a polar sled he invented (see fig. 5.1). He proceeded to carry out trials of the device with Raymond Roussel, his novelist friend.

In his book *Deux Logis Alchimiques* (Two Alchemical Abodes),[2] Champagne's disciple Eugène Canseliet published a photograph of this fabulous propeller sled that was so ahead of its time.

It was also on this street, the rue Vernier, at number 5, that the famous abbé Julio established his chapel. Robert Ambelain records this fact in his book *L'Abbé Julio*.[3]

In 1911, Bernard de Lesseps ultimately proposed that Jean-Julien Champagne come to live in a spare corner of the de Lesseps mansion on the avenue Montaigne and committed to a monthly stipend of five hundred francs for Champagne's work on the polar sled.

With the death of Félix Gaboriau[†] in that same year, Champagne lost the man who initiated him into alchemy. (Examples of Gaboriau's letters are reproduced in figure 5.3; see pages 56–57.)

---

*[Ferdinand-Marie de Lesseps supervised the building of the Suez Canal. —*Ed.*]

[†]Félix Gaboriau was born in 1861 and died in 1911. He had devoted his time and his small inheritance to the publication of a theosophical journal, *Le Lotus*.

*Fig. 5.1. Turbo-propulsion device under construction, June 1914; trial, July 1914—Jean-Julien Champagne, the avenue Montaigne*

Our painter Champagne frequented two worlds that existed side by side and intermingled. In the world of literature, for example, Anatole France, who was often invited to the de Lesseps home, was also interested in occultism and, particularly, in spiritualism. He even participated in a few séances, which left him with some rather unpleasant memories.

All these people were involved in alchemy—a fashionable pursuit of those times. Courses in hermetic science were offered by a wide range of groups.

The brothers Chacornac, friends of Dujols, also employed Champagne in their bookstore on the riverbank in Paris. His work involved receiving books coming in from private libraries, generally from the provinces, evaluating them, and shelving them. This was hardly an unpleasant task, for he was always on the lookout for old books dealing with alchemy.

Explication très Curieuse des Énigmes et Figures Hiéroglyphiques, Physiques, qui sont au Grand Portail de l'Église Cathédrale et Métropolitaine de Notre-Dame de Paris.

Par

le Sieur Esprit Gobineau de Montluisant, Gentilhomme Chartrain, Ami de la Philosophie Naturelle et Alchimique.

Le Mercredi 20 de May 1640, veille de la glorieuse Ascension de notre Sauveur Jésus-Christ, après avoir prié Dieu, et sa très-sainte Mère Vierge, en l'Église Cathédrale et Métropolitaine de Notre-Dame de Paris, je sortis de cette belle et grande Église, et considérant attentivement son riche et magnifique Portail, dont la structure est très-exquise, depuis le fondement jusqu'à la sommité de ses deux hautes et admirables Tours, je fis les remarques que je vais expliquer.

Je commence par observer que ce Portail est triple, pour former trois principales Entrées dans ce superbe Temple, seul corps de bâtiment, et au moyen la Trinité de Personnes en un seul Dieu, sous lesquelles par l'opération de son Esprit Saint, son Verbe s'est incarné pour le salut du monde dans les flancs de la Vierge sainte; symbole des trois principes célestes ensuite, qui sont les trois principales clefs ouvrant les principes, et toutes les portes, les avenues et les entrées de la nature sublunaire, c'est-à-dire de la Sève universelle, et de tous les corps qu'elle Forme et produit, conserve ou régénère.

1: La figure posée au premier cercle du Portail, vis-à-vis l'Hôtel-Dieu représente, au plus haut, Dieu le Père, créateur de l'Univers, étendant ses bras et tenant en chacune de ses mains une figure d'homme, en forme d'Ange.

Cela représente que Dieu Tout-Puissant, au moment de la création, de toutes choses, qu'il Fit de rien, séparant la lumière des ténèbres, en Fit ces nobles Créatures que les Sages appellent Âme Catholique, Esprit Universel ou Souffre vital incombustible, et Mercure de Vie; c'est-à-dire l'Humide radical général, lesquels deux principes sont figurés par ces deux Anges.

Dieu le Père les tient en ses deux mains, pour faire la distinction du souffre vital, ou huile de vie, qu'on appelle Âme, et du Mercure de vie, ou humide premier né, qu'on nomme Esprit, quoique ce soient termes synonymes, mais seulement pour faire concevoir que cette Âme et cet Esprit tirent leur principe et leur origine du monde Suréleste, et Archétypique, où est le Siège et le Thrône plein de gloire du Très-Haut, d'où il émane Surnaturellement et imperceptiblement pour se communiquer, comme la première racine, la première Âme mouvante, et la source de vie de tous les Êtres en général, et de toutes les Créatures sublunaires, dont l'homme est le chef de prédilection.

2: Dans le cercle au-dessous du monde Suréleste, et Archétypique, est le Ciel firmamental, ou Astral, dans lequel paroissent deux Anges la tête penchée, mais couverte et enveloppée.

Fig. 5.2. A sample of the handwriting of Jean-Julien Champagne

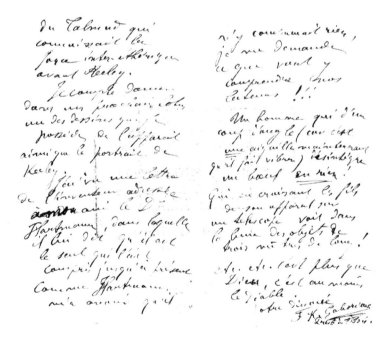

Fig. 5.3 *Letters from Gaboriau, the man who initiated Champagne.*
*(Documents kindly supplied by the Municipal Library of Lyons)*

Now it happened that one day, when he was busy classifying books, a rare copy of one of Newton's writings fell into his hands.[4] Upon opening it, he discovered a six-page manuscript from 1830 that consisted of notes taken by a researcher in the course of his experiments and articulating his success. Champagne stole these precious leaves and took them home to study them further.

Already exulting in the idea of being able to obtain a similar result for himself, he discovered to his great joy that the document spoke of alchemical manipulations leading to the famous blue and red colors that were used in the stained-glass windows of Chartres Cathedral.

From then on he delved into the manuscript and tried to decipher it, spending many hours in the laboratory, but with no success.

Then one day in 1913, while he was at the Closerie-des-Lilas, as was his custom, he noticed René Schwaller, who, he knew, had a great interest in alchemy and a strong knowledge of chemistry. Champagne approached him and proposed a reading of the manuscript he had discovered, with a view to possible collaboration.

Self-interest guided him—if he had been able to resolve the problem himself, he undoubtedly never would have shown these pages to the future Egyptologist.* Schwaller was immediately interested. Besides alchemy, René Schwaller displayed a great curiosity for theories on the composition of matter. In fact, he disapproved totally of the work on the atom, which, he was to say later, presented great dangers for humanity. This was a position he maintained all his life, and the facts have not proved him wrong.†

Schwaller's work with numbers led him to study architectural forms and the cathedrals in particular. During his stay in Paris, he often went to Notre Dame Cathedral in order to observe its architecture and sculptures. In this way, he studied the symbolism of the cathedrals and their relationship to the art of alchemy. In fact, he had drafted a manuscript on this topic.

That is why the few pages that Champagne showed him stirred him so strongly. The two men negotiated a contract: Schwaller would contrib-

---

*Moreover, during their long collaboration, they did not think much of each other, satisfied only with making the best use of each other's competencies. On this topic, consult the amazing story of Mr. André VandenBroeck in his book *Al-Kemi, a Memoir: Hermetic, Occult, Political, and Private Aspects of R. A. Schwaller de Lubicz* (Rochester, Vt., and Great Barrington, Mass.: Inner Traditions/Lindisfarne Press, 1987). The author befriended Schwaller, who, in turn, told him all the details of this surprising story.

According to the description that Schwaller gave to André VandenBroeck, the manuscript was written on stiff paper from a sketchbook, cut in octavo, yellowing at the edges. The ink was a blackish brown but had withstood the passage of time, and the leaves were soiled with spots of oil.

†In Pauwels and Bergier's *Le Matin des Magiciens* (Paris: Gallimard, 1960; English edition, *The Morning of the Magicians,* New York: Dorset Press, 1988), there is a conversation referred to between Bergier and an alchemist in a gas-testing laboratory in Paris. The researcher conveys to Bergier his warning about the nuclear reactor.

Robert Amadou in his series of articles on the Fulcanelli affair in *L'Autre Monde* (1983) discloses that Jacques Bergier, "after learning that he was terminally ill," confided to him that Fulcanelli was Schwaller de Lubicz.

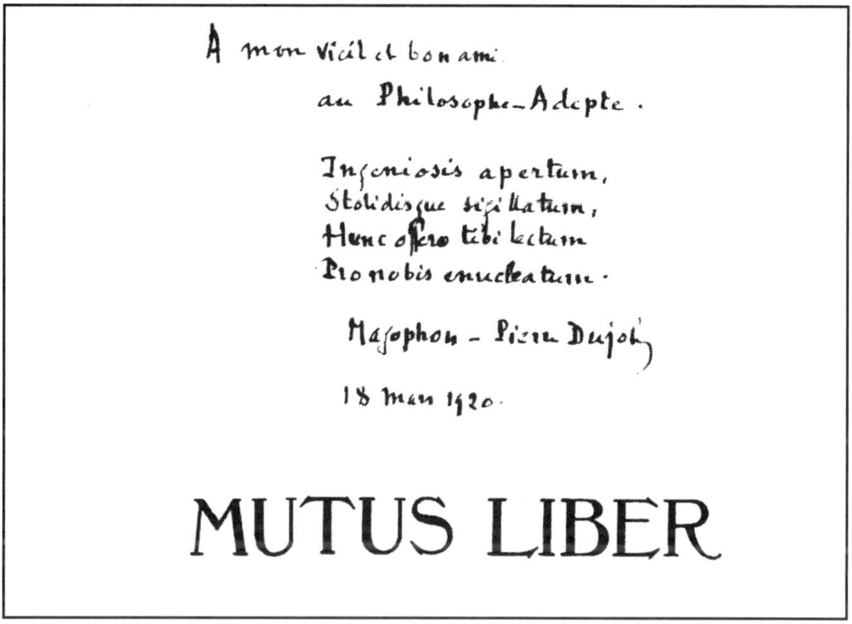

A mon vieil et bon ami

au Philosophe-Adepte.

Ingeniosis apertum,
Stolidisque sigillatum,
Hunc offro tibi lectum
Pro nobis enucleatum.

Magophon - Pierre Dujols,

18 mars 1920.

# MUTUS LIBER

*Fig. 5.4. The dedication from Pierre Dujols to Fulcanelli. Translation: "To my old and faithful friend, the Philosopher-Adept: Open to the ingenious, / And closed to fools, / I offer you this reading / For our elucidation. Magophon—Pierre Dujols, March 18, 1920"*

ute a monthly payment to the painter that would allow him to support himself and, in return, Champagne was to work on the operational aspects—Schwaller would clarify the theory and Champagne, an excellent technician in the laboratory, would carry out the experiments.

In the contract, one condition was stipulated: Whatever happened, whether they succeeded or failed, neither was to reveal the existence of this contract, and upon its expiration, the two would go their separate ways without ever mentioning the subject again.

The nonobservance of this pact was to have fatal consequences for Champagne. At least, that is how Schwaller later explained the ultimate decline of his partner.

Jean-Julien Champagne thus carried out his experiments while the upheaval of war battered France. Schwaller was mobilized to work in a military laboratory carrying out nutrition analyses; nevertheless, he continued to pursue his experiments with the alchemist. He recognized Champagne as a master, both for his erudition in alchemical symbolism and for his extraordinary mastery of the operational aspects of the science.

At the same time, Champagne continued to work at the home of the de Lesseps family, and in July 1914 the first trials of his propeller were successfully conducted.

It was quite a happy crowd that then gathered at the avenue Montaigne. Among them were certain symbolist poets such as André Breton, who was later connected with Eugène Canseliet. Champagne also regularly frequented his friend Dujols's place. Dujols was working on his introduction to the *Mutus Liber,** and the two discussed alchemy, symbolism, and the hermetic cabala.

Schwaller later told André VandenBroeck about the obsession that emanated from this group: to try and explain everything using the Greek language. Schwaller found this approach obsolete and not corresponding to our times. For him, the only cabala that was possible and contemporary was that based on Egyptian hieroglyphics.

In 1915, Eugène Canseliet was introduced to Champagne. He was sixteen years old; the painter was thirty-eight. Dujols was fifty-three and Schwaller twenty-eight. Eugène Canseliet did not hesitate to become the attentive student of this master whom he admired so much and whom he served all his life. In the first years, he acted as an assistant for Champagne's courses.

Canseliet actually became the pivot in manipulations of which he remained quite unaware—a kind of hoax that would take a turn its perpetrators did not perhaps foresee.

In fact, thanks to Champagne, Eugène Canseliet entered the worldly and occultist high society of Paris. He was often at the de Lesseps home,

---

*On page 3 of his "Hypotypose," Pierre Dujols includes an error: He writes that Dr. Girtaner declared that in the twentieth century the Chrysopoeia would be in the public domain. According to Father Migne, in his *Dictionnaire des Sciences Occultes* (1848), volume 2, column 315, the article on the philosopher's stone: "Dr. Girtaner of Göttingen recently ventured to predict that in the nineteenth century the transmutation of metals would generally be known."

at the symbolist group with André Breton, and among the little circle of Pierre Dujols, which he came to know only slightly. He did, however, forge a strong friendship with Paul Le Cour, founder of the Atlantis movement, and he refined his alchemical education, both operational and symbolic, at the feet of his master, Champagne.

If Canseliet was of prime importance in the distribution of the work of Fulcanelli, he was similarly key to the tenacious spreading of the legend. He was often seen in libraries, where, using his beautiful handwriting, he honed his skills in reproducing the calligraphy of ancient manuscripts.

Canseliet also often accompanied Champagne to the home of his mother at Arnouville-les-Gonesses, the avenue Viollet-le-Duc, where she was living at the time.

There they painted a number of canvases, including a portrait of Champagne on August 12, 1921, by Canseliet, who reproduced it in his book *L'Alchimie expliquée sur ses textes classiques* (Alchemy as Explained by Its Classic Texts).

Irène Hillel-Erlanger, a young woman who was a friend of Louis Aragon and the daughter of a rich banker, was known to have an evening drink with the Surrealists at the café on the place Blanche in Paris. She also often went to the home of the de Lessepses on the avenue Montaigne. She was born June 30, 1878, and died in Paris on March 21, 1920. One of her ancestors, Abraham de Camondo, who died in 1873, had been the banker for the sultan of Constantinople.

An occasional poet writing under the pseudonym Claude Lorrey, she left her mark for posterity with a book: In 1919, in Paris, Georges Crès published her *Voyages en Kaléidoscope,* a little pamphlet whose significance depended neither on its style nor on its storyline—which was rather ordinary—but rather on the alchemical underpinnings that shone through its text.[6]

Jean-Julien Champagne ascribed a great deal of importance to this document, in which, it seems, the Great Work is revealed. Doubtless he was no stranger to Irène. His influence with the de Lessepses in questions of alchemy was significant, and Irène was a familiar figure there. She was also a friend of Louise Barbe, to whom she dedicated her little book: "To the great soul of L. B., piously I offer these pages. I. H. E."

Louise was the first wife of Dr. Voronoff, who, according to Robert Ambelain, Champagne masterfully hoodwinked, for our painter was a prankster and a bon vivant. He convinced Serge Voronoff* that he possessed the Chrysopoeia, and to support his claim he showed Voronoff his identity card indicating that he was of a venerable age in relation to his astonishingly young physical appearance. In fact, it was his father's card, which he had pinched, for he was extremely crafty.

In 1921, Jean-Julien Champagne was invited to work on the drawings for a refrigeration plan at the Château de Léré, in the Berry region. This house belonged to Pierre de Lesseps, who was one of Ferdinand's sons. The canal builder had bought this abandoned property with money from the sale of a property located near Paris and belonging to his mother-in-law. He had the land cultivated, built a model farm, and repaired the old chateau, which had belonged to Agnès Sorel.[7]

Champagne also taught drawing and, at his convenience, continued to use the laboratory that was made available to him in order to go on with his alchemical experiments. But he stayed just a short time in the Berry region, and in 1922 he returned to Paris, where he met Jules Boucher (J. B.), who became another of his disciples.

At the time, Boucher was working at Rhône-Poulenc, and it was through a cousin of Champagne who was also employed there that the meeting between Champagne and Boucher took place.[†]

It was in this same year, 1922, during the month of September, that Eugène Canseliet, twenty-five years old, was present at the famous

---

*Serge Voronoff was the director of the laboratories at the Collège de France. In 1930, he investigated a technique of applying grafts from monkey testicles in pursuit of a "cure" for aging. He published his results: 475 grafts!

†In note 1 on page 1 of his commentary *Science écrite de tout l'Art Hermétique* (Documented Knowledge on the Complete Hermetic Art), Jules Boucher writes: "The few comments that we have added are from notes taken during conversations with our dear departed master and friend, Fulcanelli."

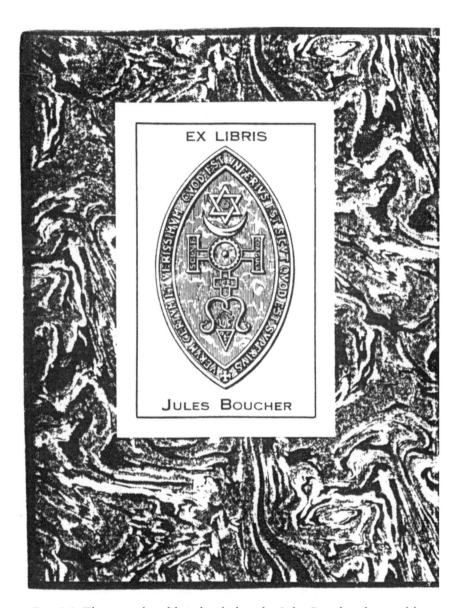

*Fig. 5.5. The second ex libris bookplate for Jules Boucher designed by Jean-Julien Champagne. Champagne's own bookplate showed a green circle with a retort.*

transmutation. He carried out the projection* himself, under Fulcanelli's direction. The scene took place in the small apartment that he occupied in the gas factory at Sarcelles in the presence of Jean-Julien Champagne and the chemist Gaston Sauvage. This transmutation was not the result of the success of the Great Work, but rather a single specific instance. Eugène Canseliet admitted it himself to the dearly departed Savoret.†

It is possible that the curious dedication addressed to Aor (René Schwaller de Lubicz) by a soldier who had taken the initiatory name Parsifal (see fig. 5.6) refers to this experiment, although the dates differ: September 1922 for Eugène Canseliet and the nights of May 9 and 10 for Parsifal. The name ELIE, which is not unknown to alchemists, appears in the dedication itself.‡

Also in 1922, René Schwaller left Paris, severing all contacts with esoteric groups, notably with the group of alchemists who had gathered around Pierre Dujols and Julien Champagne. But he continued to send Champagne the monthly allowance according to their agreement. In the book *Feu du Soleil,* by Robert Amadou, Eugène Canseliet reports that Fulcanelli left in 1922 and that he did not see him again until 1952 (the date when Schwaller returned to Europe to settle in the south of France at Plan-de-Grasse, after a stay of fifteen years in Egypt. He had left France in 1938). (See appendix C for a full chronology of René Schwaller de Lubicz.)

---

*[The term *projection* is used to refer to the catalytic event that triggers the transmutation of base metals. —*Trans.*]

†André Savoret (1898–1977), a friend of Eugène Canseliet and of Georges Richet and the alchemist known by the pseudonym Auriger, displayed an interest in druidism, having been influenced by the great thaumaturgist Philéas Lebesgue. He created the Collège Bardique des Gaules and was the author of numerous books: *Du Menhir à la Croix: Essais sur la triple tradition de l'Occident* (From the Menhir to the Cross: Essays on the Triple Tradition of the West, 1932); translations of *La Nuée sur le Sanctuaire* (Clouds over the Sanctuary) and *Essais chimiques de Eckartshausen* (Chemical Essays of Eckartshausen); *Les Forces Secrètes de la Vie* (The Secret Forces of Life, 1937); *L'Inversion Psychanalytique* (The Psychoanalytical Inversion, 1939); and *Visages du druidisme* (Faces of Druidism).

‡The movement, called Les Veilleurs [begun in 1920 by Schwaller de Lubicz], included as well an inner circle called the Ordre d'Elie (Order of Eli).

*Fig. 5.6. Photo with a dedication addressed to Aor and Isha, signed "Parsifal, November 1922"*

In 1975, in the course of a conversation in Salt Lake City, Eugène Canseliet confided to Frater Albertus that Fulcanelli had made a second transmutation in the fall of 1937. In his book *The Alchemist of the Rocky Mountains,* Frater Albertus Spagyricus (alias Albert Riedel) relates the details of the experiment that proceeded at the Château de Léré, which belonged to Pierre de Lesseps. According to him, Fulcanelli transmuted 225 grams of lead into gold and 100 grams of silver into uranium in the presence of two physicists, a chemist, and a geologist. He would have mentioned that the catalytic "powder of projection" [one form of the philosopher's stone] was derived from iron pyrites ($FeS$). After this operation, Fulcanelli disappeared permanently.

It was Kenneth Rayner Johnson, author of *The Fulcanelli Phenomenon,* who wrote to Frater Albertus asking for the source of his information.

The response he received was that it came from an interview that Frater Albertus had with Eugène Canseliet in 1975.

René Schwaller had become Schwaller de Lubicz by right of the honor to use the appellation "de Lubicz," which was bestowed on him on January 10, 1919, by the Lithuanian poet Oscar Vladislas de Lubicz Milosz (1877–1939; fig. 5.7).

The two men met in Paris in the Theosophical Society, which René Schwaller frequented from 1913 to 1916. They were both interested in heraldry and particularly in the possible relation between the coat of arms and reincarnation. When in each other's company, they called each other "brothers in arms."

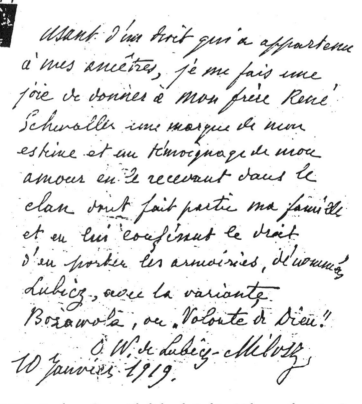

*Fig. 5.7. Letter from Oscar Vladislas de Lubicz Milosz authorizing René Schwaller to become Schwaller de Lubicz*

It was René Schwaller who revealed to Milosz the meaning of the alchemical path. In a letter dated August 10, 1936, and addressed to Dom Bernard Geradon, Milosz alludes to a certain matter known to alchemists:

> Today, following the fifth cryptographic exploration of the Two Testaments, I find myself constrained to remain silent on certain points that I have not yet communicated to the Vicar of Our Lord: the first concerns a physical substance that, so to say, has been put into my hands and that explains the *longevity* of personages included in the genealogy from Adam to Seth up to Noah and an unpublished fragment of "Deux Messianismes politiques" [Two Political Messianic Movements].
>
> It is interesting to follow people of the Middle Ages on their pilgrimages to Saint-Jacques de Compostelle and other magical sites because behind the deliberate and necessary obscurity of their allegorical relations are hidden truths, the abrupt revealing of which would risk dangerously demoralizing the two opposing camps of the faithful and the materialists. In the most natural way, these truths derive from the immediate knowledge of a certain *substance* that has been described in almost identical terms by all the ancient chemists, a substance, moreover, whose common and sacred names each of us utters every day, especially between the fall and spring equinoxes. . . . Let us add, however, before leaving this subject that the material in question resembles only very distantly the mysterious "nostoc."[8]

In 1917, Schwaller organized meetings for the exchange of opinions on different topics, which quickly evolved into purely metaphysical debates. After the end of the war (in 1919), this movement took the name Les Veilleurs (the Watchers) and was supported by Gaston Revel's journal, which changed its name from *Le Théosophe* to *Le Veilleur*. This name was inspired by the unpublished novel of Nicolas Beaudoin entitled *Les Veilleurs de la Nuit* (The Watchers of the Night). The editorial columns of the journal addressed various political and social issues, and articles were signed "Aor,"* the mystical name of René Schwaller, which he had received, according to some, by revelation, and according to others, during his time spent at the Theosophical Society. Whatever the case may be, the name means "light," and Schwaller honored it all his life.

This "fraternity of watchers" was based on an association called Le Centre Apostolique, which had as a motto "Hierarchy-Fraternity-Liberty." According to Pierre Mariel, it was really a kind of occultist synarchy (i.e., based on joint rule) supporting a political-social messianism[9] that was inspired in part by the ideas of Saint-Yves d'Alveydre, notably of the corporate movement.[10] This association was directed by a closed group otherwise called Frères de l'Ordre Mystique de la Résurrection (Brothers of the Mystical Order of the Resurrection). A journal called *l'Affranchi* published the thought of the Centre Apostolique and dealt with social questions.

Besides René Schwaller and Oscar V. Milosz, a number of people participated actively in the Fraternité des Veilleurs:

- Jeanne Germain, wife of Georges Lamy, the shipping magnate from Caen. She was better known by the *nomen mysticum* of Isha, and in 1927, after being widowed, she became the wife of René Schwaller.[11]
- Louis Allainguillaume (born in Caen, France, in 1878; died in Cardiff, Wales, in 1946), father of Isha's two sons. He was a wealthy coal merchant. René Schwaller was employed in his business and organized the finances so that its fortunes, already flourishing, soared even further. Louis Allainguillaume therefore accorded Schwaller significant dividends, which allowed the scholar to pursue his own research in complete tranquillity and to hand over to Jean-Julien Champagne a healthy sum each month.

---

*In the book by Alexandre de Danam, *Mémoire du Sang* (Milan: Arché, 1990), on page 91, we learn that the mystical name of René Schwaller was "Aor, "or more precisely" Aor Mahomet Ahliah," in order to establish a connection to the pseudonym of the alchemist Dina: A. M. A.

*Fig. 5.8. Louis Allainguillaume*

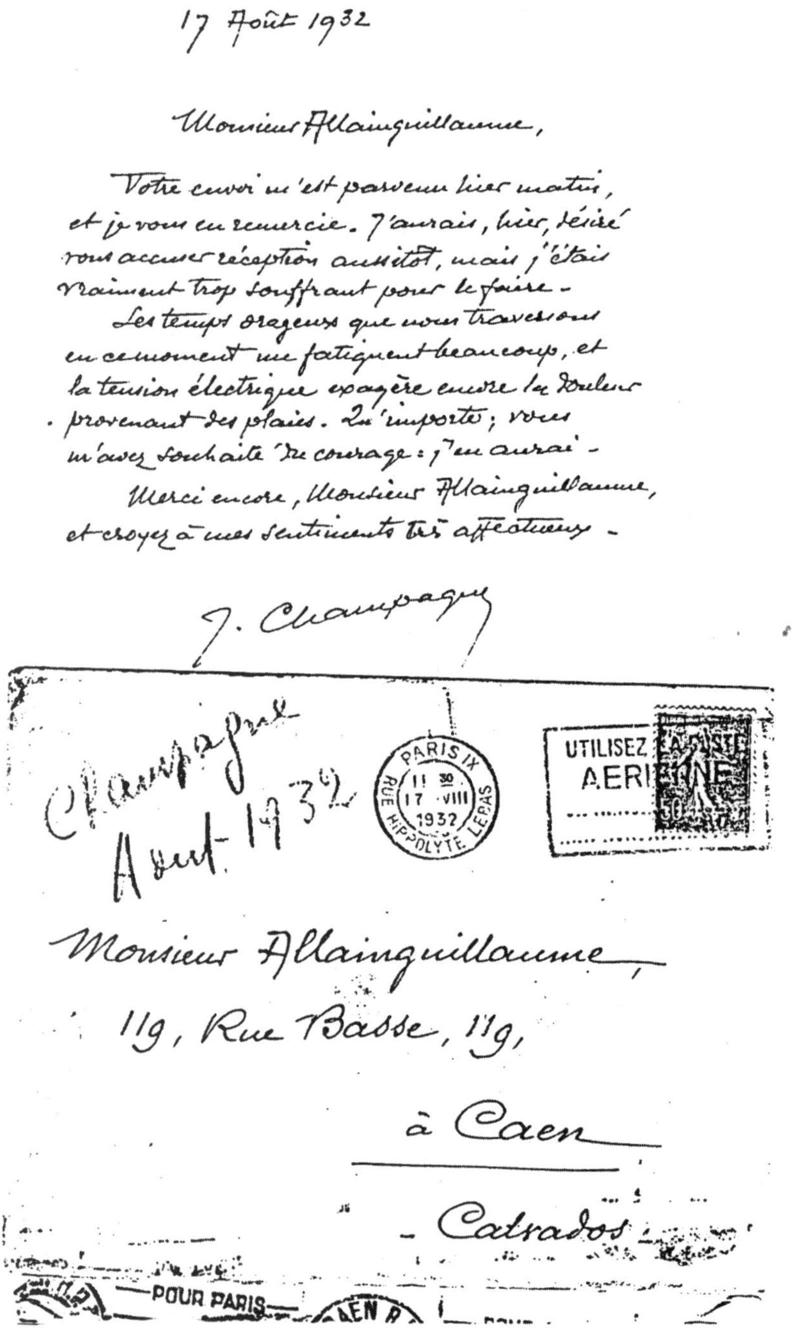

*17 Août 1932*

*Monsieur Allainguillaume,*

*Votre envoi m'est parvenu hier matin, et je vous en remercie. J'aurais, hier, désiré vous accuser réception aussitôt, mais j'étais vraiment trop souffrant pour le faire –*

*Les temps orageux que nous traversons en ce moment me fatiguent beaucoup, et la tension électrique exagère encore la douleur provenant des plaies. N'importe; vous m'avez souhaité me courage : j'en aurai –*

*Merci encore, Monsieur Allainguillaume, et croyez à mes sentiments très affectueux –*

*J. Champagne*

*Monsieur Allainguillaume,*
*119, Rue Basse, 119,*
*à Caen*
*– Calvados*

Fig. 5.9. Letter from Jean-Julien Champagne addressed to Allainguillaume

- Carlos Larronde, journalist and poet. He was a great friend of Milosz and the founder of the Théâtre Idéaliste, which, for lack of financing, had a short history (1914–17).
- The chemist and astrologer Henri Coton-Alvart, who had as a disciple Dr. Emerit. Henri Coton was born in Paris on May 6, 1894, and died in the south of France in January 1988 at the age of ninety-five. He quickly departed from this movement in order to seclude himself in a beneficial solitude that allowed him to achieve success in his alchemical endeavors. According to a witness who had known him for a period of fifteen years, he obtained the philosopher's stone.
- Gaston Revel (died in 1939). He was the founder and editor in chief of the journal *Le Théosophe*.
- Le Charpentier
- René Bruyez, who was the president of the group
- Henri Postel du Mas, who stayed only a short time

This initiatory order met in the house that belonged to Balzac on the rue Raynouard.

The outer circle of the Fraternité des Veilleurs included numerous sympathizers. Among them were Henri de Regnier, Paul Fort, Fernand Léger, Georges Polti, Pierre Benoit, and Camille Flammarion.

In 1921, Aor decided to suspend the existence of this movement as well as the journal *Le Veilleur*. According to Jacques Buge, in his interesting book on Milosz, this action was the result of the departure of Milosz, Beaudoin, Bruyez, and Larronde, who were opposed to the spiritualistic practices that had overtaken the metaphysical discussions. (See appendix D for the translation of a letter written by Schwaller to an unknown recipient that discusses Milosz, ancient Egypt, and Les Veilleurs.)

During the war years, which he spent in Paris, Schwaller had drafted a manuscript on the subject of the Gothic cathedrals, dear to his heart, and on alchemical symbolism. He showed it to Champagne, who seemed interested and suggested he submit his work to a publisher.

Because he was well connected to the publishing world, Champagne took on the task of finding one.

Schwaller, being trusting, willingly loaned his manuscript to Champagne, and Jean-Julien promised to return it quickly. He kept it, though, for several days, at the end of which time he returned it to Schwaller and advised him that the study revealed too many secrets and therefore could not be made available to just anyone.

At the time, Schwaller was preparing to leave for Engadine, Switzerland (the region around Saint-Moritz), where, accompanied by Isha and a few faithful friends, he was going to build a scientific installation called Suhalia. It was to be a kind of initiatory monastery equipped with an observatory, run by the astronomer Juvisy, and a highly advanced chemical laboratory. In addition, it would house a foundry, a print shop, and a weaving workshop supporting the development of crafts. Last, there was to be an installation to support research in physics, spectroscopy, micrography, and electricity.

Work on plants helped the group at Suhalia to develop a homeopathic pharmacopoeia with very effective tinctures. For seven years, until 1927, Aor-Schwaller taught his philosophical doctrine to members of this community. An internal document he created for the group helped him in this teaching.

During his stay in Switzerland, he regularly sent the agreed-upon allowance to Champagne for his research.

In March 1925 Champagne moved to 59A rue Rochechouart, where he occupied a very modestly furnished garret on the sixth floor. His immediate neighbor was his disciple Eugène Canseliet; the men were separated only by the washroom on their floor.

Champagne was scrupulously careful to hide his relations with Schwaller from his disciples, notably from Dujols. He had, in fact, asked Schwaller not to meet him when any of his entourage was present. In order to conform to this strategy, all the correspondence that they exchanged—even the monthly allowance sent to Champagne—was sent through Champagne's brother-in-law, Gaston Devaux, who lived in the Somme département and acted as a forwarding address for Champagne.

*Fig. 5.10. Aor and Isha at the time of their marriage in 1927*

*Fig. 5.11. Aor and Isha*

*Fig. 5.12. Isha Schwaller de Lubicz*

*Fig. 5.13. Laboratory equipment and a spectrometer belonging to Aor.
The furniture came from Palma de Mallorca.*

Fig. 5.14. Jean-Julien Champagne, age thirty-seven

In Robert Amadou's *Feu du Soleil,* Eugène Canseliet presents Gaston Devaux as "Fulcanelli's secretary." Devaux owned a ring identical to Canseliet's ring with a baphomet. Long after the death of the painter Champagne, Canseliet continued to travel to the Devaux home in the Somme.

Gaston Devaux, who died in 1969, stated in 1952 that the Fulcanelli affair was completely fabricated; a hoax. Contrary to the opinion of his descendants, Devaux was keenly interested in alchemy.

Jean-Julien Champagne had his peculiarities: He detested electricity, for example, and preferred to use oil lamps. He dressed in an outmoded fashion, sported a handlebar mustache, and wore his hair long. He gave the impression of not belonging to his own century, always buried as he was in reading ancient authors and having a fondness for the Middle Ages, which he did not consider a dark period at all.

He also had the custom of compartmentalizing his different relationships: He would meet with people belonging to different groups who never had any contact with each other. He pretended to be horrified by occultism, but attended meetings such as those of the Grand Lunaire and even those of the Veilleurs. All his life he wove the veil that was intended to establish the Fulcanelli myth. The comical aspect of this business was that at the dawn of the twentieth century, a time so full of reason, no one doubted any of this. Everyone simply latched on to these books that were full of the promise of longevity and omniscience and so on.

Champagne devoted years to maintaining the fiction of Fulcanelli's vocation as an adept. He had launched this fiction, and it was maintained by the whole group around him, all of whom must have promoted the myth: Gaston Sauvage, the Chacornacs, Pierre Dujols, Canseliet, Jules Boucher. They formed the mysterious Fraternité d'Héliopolis (F.C.H.), whose double name had perhaps been borrowed from the Belgian lodge of the Memphis-Misraïm Rite, which, in 1839, called itself Les Sages d'Héliopolis.

Eugène Canseliet placed the birth of Fulcanelli in 1839, the year of the establishment of this lodge. This was a gesture, a reference, a broad wink in the direction of the eminently Freemasonic circle around Pierre

Dujols and Champagne. Thomas,* an associate of the bookstore owner and of the painter, had this affiliation, as did Oswald Wirth, Guénon, Chacornac, Marc Haven, Boucher, and Ferdinand de Lesseps, in whose honor the Masonic feast was given in 1876. It is probable that the de Lesseps children also belonged to the Freemasonry movement.

In 1880, Pierre Dujols had been bedridden with rheumatoid arthritis for four years already. Because of a tenuous financial situation, his wife found herself obliged to work in order to subsidize the needs of the family. No one came forward to help them. Champagne brought them some money from time to time, but he often spent it drinking on the way there.

The Librairie du Merveilleux was sold. Dujols was succeeded by a Father Lequesne, a bookstore dealer, initiate, radiologist, and healer who used spiritual magnetism. In the back of his shop was an oratory full of paintings and statues.[12]

During his long years in bed, Pierre Dujols devoted his time to writing copious notes on alchemical symbolism. He shared with Champagne a veneration of Basile Valentin and Flamel. They worked on the traditional path and were preoccupied with the notion of SEL.†

Champagne traveled and, in the course of his moving around, undertook to reproduce sculptures that seemed to him to have arisen from an alchemical intent.[13] This is how he came to design the caissons of the Lallemant Hotel while he was staying near Bourges and living at the chateau of the de Lesseps family at Léré.

In the département of the Somme, he investigated the cathedral at Amiens and fairly regularly stayed with his sister, who lived in the département along with her husband, Gaston Devaux.

---

*In 1896, Alberic Thomas was honorary officer "G. des SC." of the Grand Misraïm Lodge (Egyptian Masonry) located at 42 rue Rochechouart, while he himself lived at 10 rue Durand-Claye. In 1896, at this number of this street, we find four of the thirty-nine active members of this lodge.

†[In translating the French *sel* here to the corresponding English word *salt*, we would further obscure the underlying meaning. Fulcanelli in *Le Mystère des Cathédrales* notes that the French *sel* is a homophone of *scel*, meaning "seal." —*Trans.*]

He also traveled to Limoux, where, accompanied by his faithful disciple Eugène Canseliet, he visited the cathedral of Notre Dame in Marceille.

Dujols and Champagne set to work on Schwaller's notes on the cathedral of Notre Dame in Paris and in particular on its relation to hermetic science. Dujols brought to this endeavor his remarkable learning and Champagne contributed his talent as a designer and engineer.*

They restructured the work, enlarged it, layering it with their prodigious knowledge in the field, and Champagne confided the whole content to Eugène Canseliet in order to support the purported existence of the mysterious adept.

This is how it came about that, on June 15, 1926, *Le Mystère des Cathédrales* was published, by Jean Schémit in Paris, under the pseudonym Fulcanelli, and to the considerable amazement of Schwaller, who was at the time at Suhalia in Switzerland.

He recognized his work—the work that he had loaned to Champagne in the years 1920–22. Later he said to André VandenBroeck, "I've been taken by Fulcanelli, my ideas have been taken; well, at least now it's written down."[14] He always called Champagne Fulcanelli.

As for Pierre Dujols, it is not clear that he was ever informed of the provenance of the notes that Champagne presented to him. He was a very pious man and apparently a man of great integrity.

The spiritual quest that Schwaller was pursuing was such that he did not take Champagne to task for his thieving, and he even continued to send him the agreed-upon allowance while Jean-Julien Champagne, in his laboratory, concentrated on the resolution of the problem of colors in the stained-glass windows at Chartres. But he was completely unsuccessful.

On April 19 of the same year, 1926, Pierre Dujols died in Paris (see fig. 5.15). His wife withdrew to live with her children, separating herself completely from Jean-Julien Champagne, to whom, however, she was

---

*The chemist Mr. Coton-Alvart always maintained that *Le Mystère des Cathédrales* was written by Pierre Dujols. He had seen it at Dujols's home.

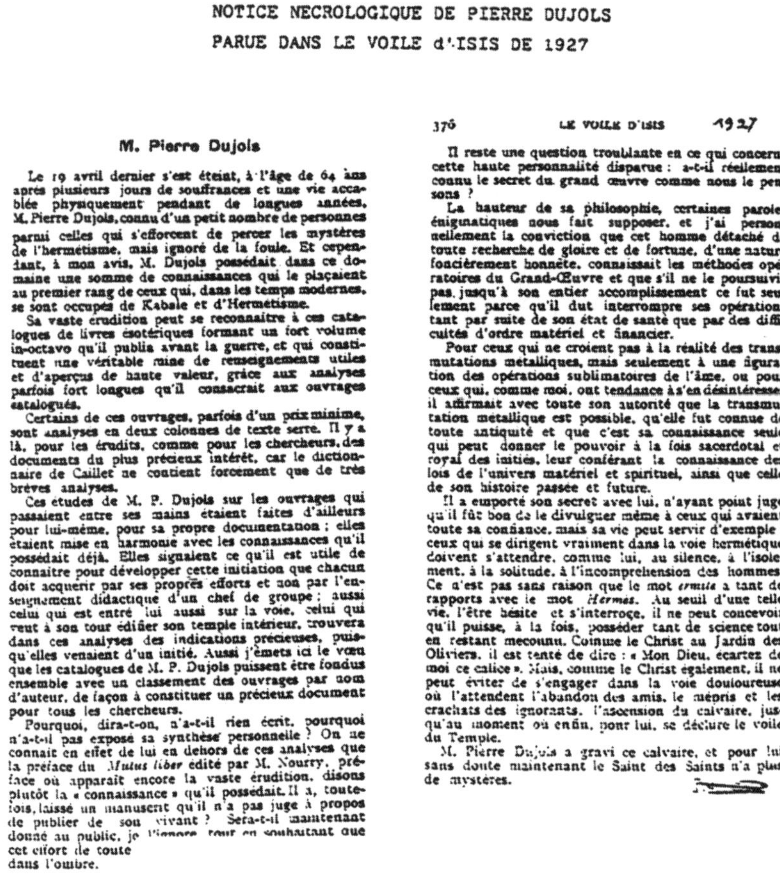

NOTICE NECROLOGIQUE DE PIERRE DUJOLS
PARUE DANS LE VOILE d'ISIS DE 1927

### M. Pierre Dujols

Le 19 avril dernier s'est éteint, à l'âge de 64 ans après plusieurs jours de souffrances et une vie accablée physiquement pendant de longues années, M. Pierre Dujols, connu d'un petit nombre de personnes parmi celles qui s'efforcent de percer les mystères de l'hermétisme, mais ignoré de la foule. Et cependant, à mon avis, M. Dujols possédait dans ce domaine une somme de connaissances qui le plaçaient au premier rang de ceux qui, dans les temps modernes, se sont occupés de Kabale et d'Hermétisme.

Sa vaste érudition peut se reconnaître à ces catalogues de livres ésotériques formant un fort volume in-octavo qu'il publia avant la guerre, et qui constituent une véritable mine de renseignements utiles et d'aperçus de haute valeur, grâce aux analyses parfois fort longues qu'il consacrait aux ouvrages catalogués.

Certains de ces ouvrages, parfois d'un prix minime, sont analysés en deux colonnes de texte serré. Il y a là, pour les érudits, comme pour les chercheurs, des documents du plus précieux intérêt, car le dictionnaire de Caillet ne contient forcément que de très brèves analyses.

Ces études de M. P. Dujols sur les ouvrages qui passaient entre ses mains étaient faites d'ailleurs pour lui-même, pour sa propre documentation ; elles étaient mise en harmonie avec les connaissances qu'il possédait déjà. Elles signalent ce qu'il est utile de connaître pour développer cette initiation que chacun doit acquérir par ses propres efforts et non par l'enseignement didactique d'un chef de groupe ; aussi celui qui est entré lui aussi sur la voie, celui qui veut à son tour édifier son temple intérieur, trouvera dans ces analyses des indications précieuses, puisqu'elles venaient d'un initié. Aussi j'émets ici le vœu que les catalogues de M. P. Dujols puissent être fondus ensemble avec un classement des ouvrages par nom d'auteur, de façon à constituer un précieux document pour tous les chercheurs.

Pourquoi, dira-t-on, n'a-t-il rien écrit. pourquoi n'a-t-il pas exposé sa synthèse personnelle ? On ne connaît en effet de lui en dehors de ces analyses que la préface du *Mutus liber* édité par M. Nourry, préface où apparaît encore la vaste érudition. disons plutôt la « connaissance » qu'il possédait. Il a, toutefois, laissé un manuscrit qu'il n'a pas juge à propos de publier de son vivant ? Sera-t-il maintenant donné au public, je l'ignore tout en souhaitant que cet effort de toute dans l'ombre.

376    LE VOILE D'ISIS    1927

Il reste une question troublante en ce qui concerne cette haute personnalité disparue : a-t-il réellement connu le secret du grand œuvre comme nous le pensons ?

La hauteur de sa philosophie, certaines paroles énigmatiques nous fait supposer, et j'ai personnellement la conviction que cet homme détaché de toute recherche de gloire et de fortune, d'une nature foncièrement honnête, connaissait les méthodes opératoires du Grand-Œuvre et que s'il ne le poursuivit pas, jusqu'à son entier accomplissement ce fut seulement parce qu'il dut interrompre ses opérations tant par suite de son état de santé que par des difficultés d'ordre matériel et financier.

Pour ceux qui ne croient pas à la réalité des transmutations métalliques, mais seulement à une figuration des opérations sublimatoires de l'âme, ou pour ceux qui, comme moi, ont tendance à s'en désintéresser il affirmait avec toute son autorité que la transmutation métallique est possible, qu'elle fut connue de toute antiquité et que c'est sa connaissance seule qui peut donner le pouvoir à la fois sacerdotal et royal des initiés, leur conférant la connaissance des lois de l'univers matériel et spirituel, ainsi que celle de son histoire passée et future.

Il a emporté son secret avec lui, n'ayant point jugé qu'il fût bon de le divulguer même à ceux qui avaient toute sa confiance, mais sa vie peut servir d'exemple : ceux qui se dirigent vraiment dans la voie hermétique doivent s'attendre, comme lui, au silence, à l'isolement, à la solitude, à l'incompréhension des hommes. Ce n'est pas sans raison que le mot *ermite* a tant de rapports avec le mot *Hermès*. Au seuil d'une telle vie, l'être hésite et s'interroge, il ne peut concevoir qu'il puisse, à la fois, posséder tant de science tout en restant méconnu. Comme le Christ au Jardin des Oliviers, il est tenté de dire : « Mon Dieu, écartez de moi ce calice ». Mais, comme le Christ également, il ne peut éviter de s'engager dans la voie douloureuse où l'attendent l'abandon des amis, le mépris et les crachats des ignorants, l'ascension du calvaire, jusqu'au moment où enfin, pour lui, se déchire le voile du Temple.

M. Pierre Dujols a gravi ce calvaire, et pour lui sans doute maintenant le Saint des Saints n'a plus de mystères.

*Fig. 5.15. Pierre Dujols's obituary notice, which appeared in the 1927 Voile d'Isis. See appendix E for a translation of this obituary.*

still very connected. Henceforth, she received visits only from Faugeron, the disciple of her husband in alchemy.

Earlier, she had given him all Dujols's alchemical files and the notes about monuments having a hermetic character. Pierre Dujols had composed many long pages on this topic, and Eugène Canseliet assembled them and submitted them to Champagne, who, in the end, presented the whole document to the publisher Schémit. Thus, in 1930, the first edition of *Les Demeures Philosophales* was offered to the public.

The family members of Pierre Dujols de Valois were astonished by the complete break of their forebear from this milieu and, above all, from Champagne.

We might assume that the alchemist had perhaps revealed the true origin of *Le Mystère des Cathédrales,* a manuscript stolen from Schwaller and augmented by Pierre Dujols. As it turned out, this book was considered by Champagne to be imperfect.

In 1929, Champagne traveled to the south of France, having been invited there by Schwaller, who was living at Lou-Mas-de-Coucagno in Plan-de-Grasse. Schwaller's invitation was addressed to a certain Mr. Hubert.

It was in regard to this name that a debate arose between Eugène Canseliet and Robert Ambelain, with Ambelain claiming that Champagne had called himself Hubert and that Hubert was the first name of Champagne's father and Canseliet disagreeing. This bitter exchange was related to the interpretation by Robert Ambelain of the closing chord of *Le Mystère des Cathédrales,* for we find on the last page of that book the inscription UBER CAMPA AGNA, or, phonetically, Hubert Champagne, which reveals that Robert Ambelain was right: Champagne did indeed have the first name Hubert, which his death certificate in fact records (fig. 5.16).

If we remember, he had pinched the identity card of his father, whose first name was also Hubert, taking it as his own in order to pass

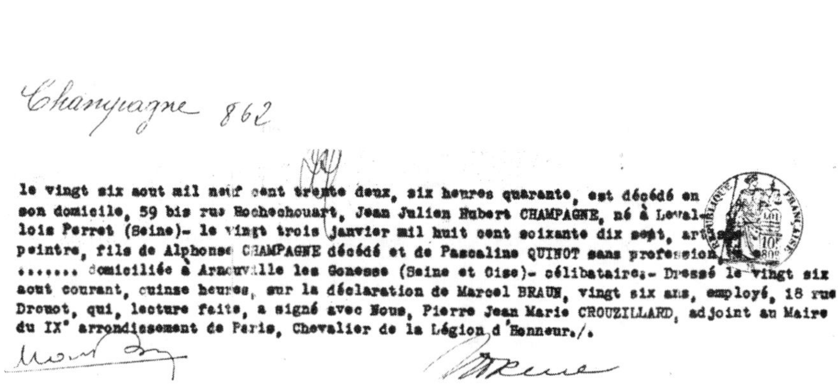
Champagne 862

le vingt six aout mil neuf cent trente deux, six heures quarante, est décédé en son domicile, 59 bis rue Rochechouart, Jean Julien Hubert CHAMPAGNE, né à Levallois Perret (Seine)- le vingt trois janvier mil huit cent soixante dix sept, artiste peintre, fils de Alphonse CHAMPAGNE décédé et de Pascaline QUINOT sans profession, ...... domiciliée à Arnouville les Gonesse (Seine et Oise)- célibataire.- Dressé le vingt six aout courant, quinze heures, sur la déclaration de Marcel BRAUN, vingt six ans, employé, 18 rue Drouot, qui, lecture faite, a signé avec Nous, Pierre Jean Marie CROUZILLARD, adjoint au Maire du IX° arrondissement de Paris, Chevalier de la Légion d'Honneur./.

*Fig. 5.16. Jean-Julien Champagne's death certificate*

for an age that his appearance belied. In this way Robert Ambelain demonstrated that Fulcanelli was Champagne and that Champagne had signed his book in a cabalistic manner.

During his stay at the home of the Schwaller de Lubicz family in Plan-de-Grasse (fig. 5.17), Champagne exchanged ideas with Aor while strolling on the broad avenue that led to the house. In memory of this time, it came to be called the Allée des philosophes, "Philosophers' Walk" (see fig. 5.18).

The men conversed about the theory and practice of the alchemical Great Work and Champagne carried out experiments in the highly advanced laboratory that René Schwaller had installed in his house.

Steadily, Schwaller established the doctrine that was drawn from the study of the manuscript on colors. The two were close to success.

Lucie Lamy, the daughter-in-law of René Schwaller, did not think much of the alchemist. Later she said as much, explaining that he behaved in an obnoxious manner and that he was very taken by drink. In fact, he did not correspond at all to her idea of a philosopher.

*Fig. 5.17. Lou-Mas-de-Coucagno, property of René (Aor) and Jeanne (Isha) Schwaller de Lubicz at Plan-de-Grasse*

*Fig. 5.18. L'Allée des Philosophes (the Philosophers' Walk), called this by Schwaller de Lubicz in memory of the visit of J.-J. Champagne*

It is during this period that René Schwaller drew a portrait of his collaborator: a drawing in red ink in which Champagne appears with long hair, as he liked to wear it. The work is dated 1930 and carries on the back the annotation "Fulcanelli" (see fig. 5.19).

The architect who was in charge of the renovation of the house that was the property of René Schwaller and which was bought back from him by Jean Lamy in monthly payments (Lucy Lamy bought a property near Thoronet) was often invited, along with his wife, to dine and spend the evening at the Schwaller home. He shares some of his reminiscences:

During the meals, in the dining room where there hung a chandelier constructed with the glass of Chartres (blues and reds), Aor loved to teach.

*Fig. 5.19. Drawing of Jean-Julien Champagne, in red ink, by René Schwaller de Lubicz, February 1930*

*Fig. 5.20. René Schwaller de Lubicz*

His daughter-in-law, Lucie, did not have the right to interrupt, nor, by the way, the right to leave the house. She lived as a recluse. Her long stay in Egypt had scorched her face and prematurely aged her. She was just there, self-effacing, although she had a very great talent for drawing and would have been justified in putting herself forward more.

Isha was just the opposite. She was very distinguished, a great lady, always well dressed. Aor regarded her highly, calling her "my great friend." The decoration of her bedroom was theatrical, with a canopy bed and also an armchair, specially designed, she said, to enable her to recharge.

Aor was an extremely gifted and intelligent being. He believed in everything mysterious. His work in Egypt had made him known throughout the world. The architect recalls:

> . . . [I]n Pennsylvania, when Aor was at the university, the community of official Egyptologists made fun of him because his method was linked to the pseudoscience of the Egyptians. His son-in-law, Jean Lamy, was a medical doctor who was a sensitive diagnostician. He prescribed homeopathic medicines using tinctures that had been developed at Suhalia and used an apparatus invented by René Schwaller: the phonophoresis.[15]
>
> His office was on the third floor of the house. He occupied three rooms that stank of cigarettes from his excessive smoking. In fact he died from too much smoking.
>
> In the countryside, he was much loved for his exactitude and for his unselfishness. Often he would accept no money from those in need. It was he who in the latter years supported the whole household. As a result, he was saddened by the fact that he had been unable to assemble the few million centimes required to publish the books of his father-in-law.
>
> After the death of his parents, he married a young woman who gave birth to a son, Jean-Christophe.

A disciple of Isha who lived for a few years near this exceptional family also offers insights into Schwaller: According to her, Aor was a man of advanced spiritual quality who showed great kindness to everyone and whose telepathic abilities could not be doubted. Although he attached no importance to it, for he was very humble, he had the ability to anticipate everyone's questions and to respond to them in a subtle way.

As for his alchemical work, it seemed not to be Aor's principal activity. He was first and foremost an "inspired" Egyptologist whose work, still not understood by official academia, nevertheless shows that he had a total understanding of the sacred science of the Egyptians.

His wife Isha had had a very trying life and had overcome all her difficulties. It was the result of her revelations on two occasions that allowed him to discover the sacred alphabet of the Egyptians. Her existence, as well as that of Aor, was devoted to the transmission of this knowledge.

We should recall, however, that Isha did not know René Schwaller when he was very close to Jean-Julien Champagne.

After his time in the south of France, Champagne returned for a few months to Paris, then, in 1930, was called back to Plan-de-Grasse. His suitcase still carried the tags for his trips south.

That same year, 1930, René Schwaller and Jean-Julien Champagne were positioned to solve the problem whose solution they had been pursuing for nineteen years: that of the fabrication of the blues and reds of the stained-glass windows of, for instance, Chartres Cathedral—certainly no small feat.

Aor understood the theory. According to Mr. VandenBroeck, he imposed a severe protocol, based on draconian conditions, that was set to result in success for the operation. Champagne plunged into the work and, following Schwaller's directives combined with his own extraordinary mastery, which everyone recognized, he began the experiment.* It was a success, as René Schwaller was to confirm later to Mr. VandenBroeck:

---

*According to Isha's disciple Th. C., it was Schwaller, not Champagne, who labored in the laboratory to accomplish this decisive operation. She also recalls that during his stay in Egypt, René Schwaller had been present at a transmutation carried out by an African alchemist on the border of Nubia (now northeastern Sudan).

He described for me the separation of sulfur carried out on copper. A colored luminosity spread over the cinders of the material. The tinting mass represented the essential dyeing within the colored glass.[16]

The Chartres glass is dyed in its mass by the volatile spirit of metals.

The famous letter published by Eugène Canseliet in the preface to the second edition of *Le Mystère des Cathèdrales* (1957) and attributed to Fulcanelli actually outlines this operation and speaks of its success.

Dear Old Friend:

This time you have truly received *God's Gift;* it is a great grace, and for the first time I understand how rare this favor is. I consider in fact that within its unfathomable depths of simplicity, the Arcanum cannot be found by the force of reason alone, no matter how subtle or trained [this reason] might be. At last you have the *Treasure of Treasures,* and let us give thanks to the Divine Light that has made you a participant in it. You have, by the way, justly deserved it through your unshakable trust in Truth, your constancy of effort, your perseverance in sacrifice, and also, let us not forget . . . *through your good works.*

When my wife told me this good news, I was dumbfounded by joyful surprise and I was beside myself with happiness, so much so that I said to myself: Let's hope that this hour of intoxication is not paid for by some dreadful tomorrow. But although I was informed only in summary fashion of the event, I believe I have understood, and this reassures me in the certainty that *the fire does not die until the Work is done and until the entire tinting mass impregnates the glass, which, from one decantation to the next, remains absolutely saturated and becomes as luminous as the sun. . . .*

It was also in the year 1930, on September 15, that the second book by Fulcanelli-Champagne was offered to the public: *Les Demeures Philosophales et le Symbolisme Hermétique dans Ses Rapports avec l'Art Sacré et l'Ésotérisme du Grand-Oeuvre* (The Dwellings of the Philosophers and Hermetic Symbolism in Their Relationship to the Sacred Art and the Esotericism of the Great Work),[17] which was the work of both Champagne and Pierre Dujols before his death. Eugène Canseliet had the role of simply assembling the notes. Later, after the death of his master Champagne, Canseliet ventured to expand the republished editions.

Once again, according to Mr. VandenBroeck, after this conclusive experiment, Champagne changed completely. He returned to Paris in a state of great excitement, completely set on continuing along this path and repeating this operation.

As Champagne and Schwaller had agreed in their earlier contract, the monthly allowance was to end at this point and all trace of an association between Schwaller and Champagne was to be effaced. This experiment had put the finishing touches on their break from one another.

For a year, Champagne kept his word and made no allusion to their laboratory work. In a letter* addressed to René Schwaller a year after the death of the painter, Eugène Canseliet conveys his disappointment in having been kept at a distance: "Might it not be that Mr. Champagne has once again shown, with respect to this material aspect of your work, a memory lapse that is as surprising as it is incomprehensible . . . ?"

In this period of separation, Julien Champagne was gravely ill: He limped, drank absinthe, and inhaled galbanum to induce visions. He took tinctures to address his illnesses, but it was too late.

At this point, according to Mr. VandenBroeck, Champagne wanted to reveal all to his disciples. In addition, in 1931 he asked René Schwaller by letter to come to Paris for a very important declaration he had to communicate to him.

When they met in a little suburban restaurant, Champagne announced his intention to reveal everything about their work, but Schwaller reminded him of their pact and, in exchange for his silence, offered to continue to help him financially.

---

*See, fig. 6.1, page 102, and appendix F.

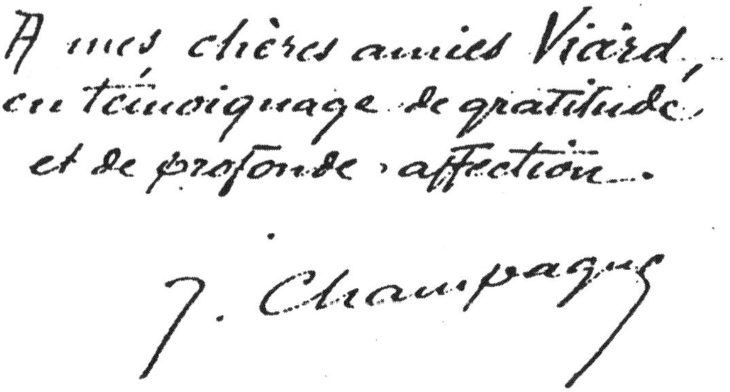
A mes chères amies Viard,
en témoignage de gratitude
et de profonde affection...

J. Champagne

*Fig. 5.21. Dedication by Jean-Julien Champagne to his friends the Viards*

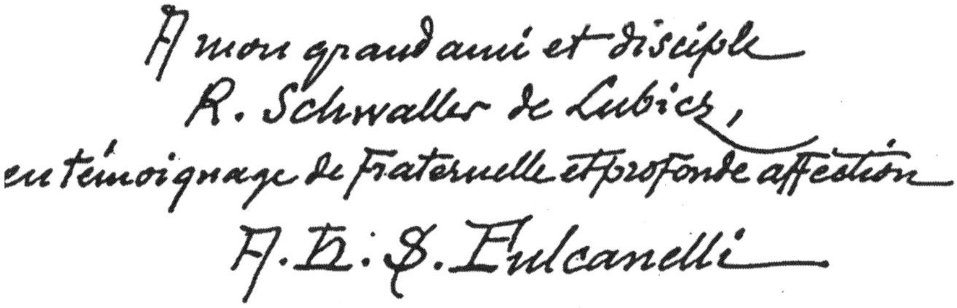
A mon grand ami et disciple
R. Schwaller de Lubicz,
en témoignage de Fraternelle et profonde affection
A.H.S. Fulcanelli

*Fig. 5.22. Dedication of Fulcanelli to R. Schwaller. Note the similarity of the handwriting of these two dedications.*

*Fig. 5.23. Jean-Julien Champagne as an old man*

In August of 1932, a very weak Champagne sent another letter to Schwaller, specifying a date that had been fixed for a meeting with his disciples.

Still according to Mr. VandenBroeck, it was a few days before this fateful date that René Schwaller returned to Paris, climbed up straight-away to the alchemist's garret at 59A rue Rochechouart, and found him in bed. Champagne's skin was black: Gangrene had spread through his leg.

Champagne must have considered the situation and, stung by remorse, pointed Schwaller toward a pile of papers, asking him to take with him the manuscript that was to be found there—the manuscript that had begun their long collaboration.

This was their last meeting, for the next day, August 26, 1932, at 6:40 A.M., Jean-Julien Champagne died at the age of fifty-five from a blocked artery in his left leg. He had not succeeded in producing the philosopher's stone, the search of his lifetime.

His sister, Mrs. Gaston Devaux, came to his room, took away some papers, and, to her amazement, discovered enough money to contradict the rumor that his end had taken place in penury. She had believed her brother was penniless and thus often gave him money.

Three days after Marcel Braun performed the registration of death (see fig. 5.24), Jean-Julien Champagne, this uncommon individual belonging to another century, was taken to his final resting place, the cemetery of Arnouville-les-Gonesse (see fig. 5.25).

His brother-in-law, Gaston Devaux, whom Eugène Canseliet claimed was Fulcanelli's secretary, took care of the funeral and the plot.*

On the grave there appears this epitaph: APOSTOLUS HERMETICAE SCIENTIAE. The initials A. H. S. are part of Fulcanelli's signature and stand for Apostle of Hermetic Science.

---

*Section D, Number 45, Cemetery of Arnouville-les-Gonesse (Seine-et-Oise). In his offprint "La Tour Saint-Jacques" (1962), Mr. Robert Ambelain puts the death of J.-J. Champagne in Paris in the Broussais Hospital, though in a later letter addressed to me he willingly takes note of his mistake, saying his information had come from Jules Boucher, who, it turns out, was at Saint-Étienne at the time of his master Champagne's death.

# M

Vous êtes prié d'assister à l'Inhumation de

# Monsieur Julien CHAMPAGNE

décédé à Paris, le 26 Août 1932, en son domicile, 59 bis, Rue de Rochechouart, à l'âge de 55 ans ;

Qui aura lieu le Lundi 29 courant, à *9 heures 15 précises,* au Cimetière d'Arnouville-les-Gonesse (Seine-et-Oise).

**REGRETS !**

## On se réunira à la porte du Cimetière

De la part de Madame veuve CHAMPAGNE, sa mère ;

De Monsieur et Madame Félix CHAMPAGNE, leurs enfants et petits-enfants, de Monsieur et Madame Gaston DEVAUX, ses frère, sœur, beau-frère, belle-sœur, neveux, nièces, petits-neveux et petites-nièces ;

De Monsieur et Madame Charles de SAINT-ACHEUL, leurs enfants et petits-enfants, ses oncle, tante, cousins et cousines ;

Et de toute la famille.

Moyen de Communication : Gare du Nord, train de 8 heures 05, descendre à Villiers-le-Bel - Gonesse.

*La levée du Corps aura lieu le Lundi 29 Août au domicile mortuaire à 8 heures 15.*

Maison Georges TROUVAIN, 18, Rue Drouot, Paris. Téléphone Taitbout 85-66

*Fig. 5.24. Announcement of the death of Jean-Julien Champagne*

*Fig. 5.25. Grave of Jean-Julien Champagne at Arnouville-les-Gonesse (Seine-et-Oise).*

*The plaque bearing the inscription* APOSTOLUS HERMETICAE SCIENTIAE *(Apostle of Hermetic Science) has disappeared, apparently either purposely removed or stolen, but the photo on page 94 shows the plaque in place.*

Champagne's sister Renée sent a letter of thanks to René Schwaller de Lubicz on September 21, 1932. From this letter we learn that it was Aor who paid for the enclosure and the tombstone of "his old friend" (fig. 5.26, pages 96–99).

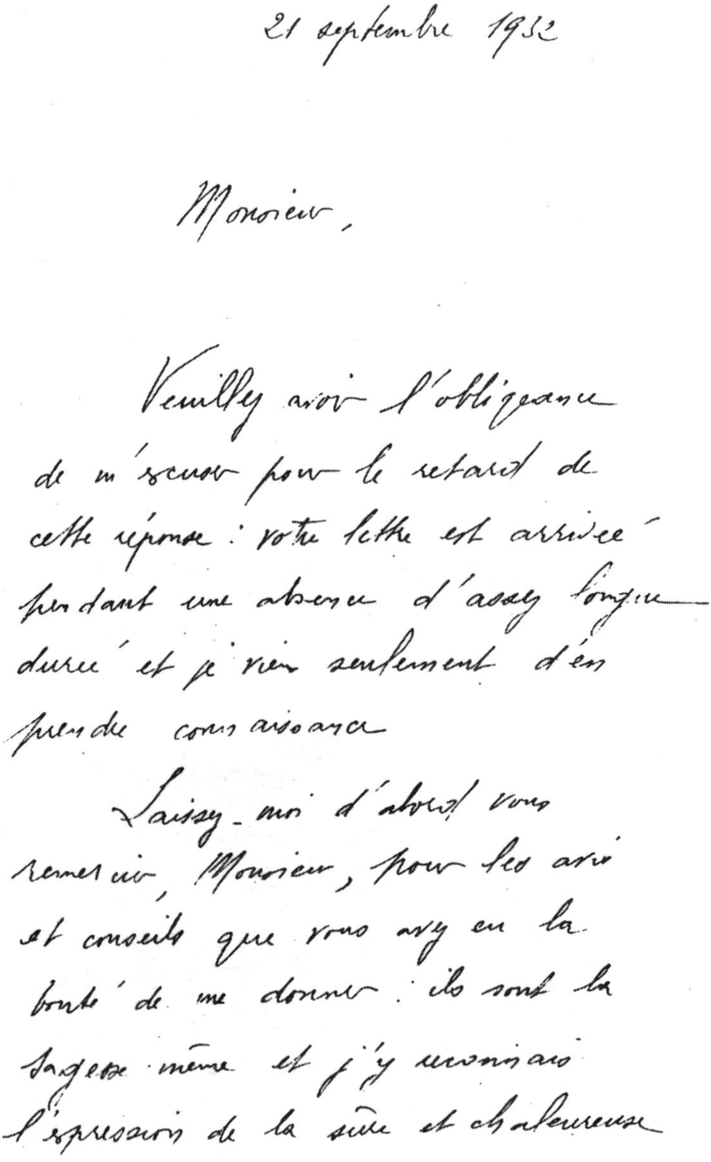

*21 septembre 1932*

*Monsieur,*

*Veuillez avoir l'obligeance de m'excuser pour le retard de cette réponse : votre lettre est arrivée pendant une absence d'assez longue durée et je viens seulement d'en prendre connaissance.*

*Laissez-moi d'abord vous remercier, Monsieur, pour les avis et conseils que vous avez eu la bonté de me donner : ils sont la sagesse même et j'y reconnais l'expression de la sûre et chaleureuse*

Fig. 5.26. *Letter from Champagne's sister Renée to René Schwaller, thanking him for her brother's tombstone. Note the epitaph on page 100.*

amitié que vous accordiez à notre
cher et regretté Hubert.

J'aurais donc été contenté de
vous être agréable et d'accéder à
tous vos désirs concernant l'inhumation
et le sépulture de mon frère. Mais
il a exigé, pour l'une, le minimum
de frais et d'ostentation; pour l'autre
une simplicité que l'on peut qualifier
d'extrême.

« Je désirerais que l'on me portât en terre dans
l'appareil le plus simple et avec le moins de
frais possible ... Que l'on place mon cadavre dans
une fosse temporaire, à même l'argile ... Un
simple et modeste entourage, quelques fleurs
pour envapper la tombe, c'est là tout ce que je
souhaite. Ne murez pas mon corps dans un
caveau = je hais la pierre humide, rigide

« fonde des in pace, et le sepulcre me
paraîtrait une prison. »

Nous avons dû nous incliner
devant une volonté si nettement
exprimée. J'ai cependant tenu à assurer
à mon cher Hubert un abri immuable
dans les concessions à perpétuité du
petit cimetière où il désirait reposer.
Mais cela était peu de chose, et la
somme dépensée pour le conduire à
sa dernière demeure ayant été
modeste, je désire qu'elle reste à
notre charge.

Mais, comprenant et appréciant
la délicatesse de votre sentiment, je
ne veux pas le heurter davantage : vous
pourrez donc, Monsieur, offrir à votre
vieil ami l'entourage qu'il souhaitait
pour sa tombe, ainsi que la pierre

ou le marbre sur lequel sera Tracée
l'inscription suivante :

Ici repose —

Apostolus Hermeticae Scientiæ
1877 – 1932.

Le tout ne pourra guère être
exécuté, je crois, avant le printemp
prochain, à cause des gelées.

Veuillez agréer, Monsieur,
avec tous mes remerciements, l'expression
de mes bons sentiments

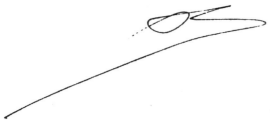

In 1938, René Schwaller de Lubicz left Lou-Mas-de-Coucagno to settle in Luxor with his whole family. He was to spend fifteen years in Egypt (fourteen of which were in Luxor itself) devoted to the study of pharaonic monuments. Upon his return to Plan-de-Grasse, he assembled his notes with the help of Lucie, who was talented at drawing, and, in 1957, finally published *Le Temple de l'Homme*.[18]

It was not until the visit of André VandenBroeck to Grasse in 1959 that Schwaller consented to reveal the relationship that he had maintained with Champagne and the alchemical work they had done together.

Corroborating what the author has to say in *Al-Kemi, a Memoir: Hermetic, Occult, Political, and Private Aspects of R. A. Schwaller de Lubicz* is evidence from researchers who knew René Schwaller well during the time of Les Veilleurs.

Aor died on December 7, 1961, at Plan-de-Grasse, followed by his wife, Isha, a year later in Paris.

Copiapite

Essential oil

Vinegar

Glass

Talc

# 6

# THE LEGEND TAKES ROOT: EUGÈNE CANSELIET, GUARDIAN OF THE MYTH

Pierre Dujols had died in 1926 and Jean-Julien Champagne in 1932. Thus Champagne's disciple Eugène Canseliet, who was later called "the Master of Savignies," undertook to establish the alchemical resurgence of the twentieth century. He had extensive experience in the laboratory, but undoubtedly spent a great deal of time shoring up the myth of Fulcanelli's vocation as an adept.

It seems that despite the numerous contradictions found in Eugène Canseliet's writings about the details of his life in association with Fulcanelli and of Fulcanelli's identity, Canseliet was the object of manipulations of which he was too young to be aware. Some people, however, do not accept this theory.

In addition, it seems that Eugène Canseliet sincerely believed that behind Jean-Julien Champagne there was another man, the master, the initiator.

The facts and the letter Canseliet wrote to René Schwaller after Champagne's death (see fig. 6.1) indicate that he was well

101

Subacetate of copper

Paris le 4 décembre 1933.

Monsieur,

Il est possible que mon nom, tracé au dos de l'enveloppe, ne vous soit pas absolument inconnu, puisque, très lié avec M. Champagne dans les dernières années de sa vie, vous avez pu quelquefois entendre parler de moi. Depuis sa mort, je poursuis seul le but d'une collaboration vieille de sept ans, qui nous fit louer, au mois de janvier 1925, deux mansardes voisines, au 59 bis de la rue de Rochechouart. Or, j'ai eu la chance et le plaisir de recevoir en prêt ces jours derniers un livre très intéressant: Adam l'homme rouge, et d'apprendre ainsi ce qu'avait omis de me dire notre ami commun: que vous êtes l'auteur de ce curieux et savant ouvrage. Vous y témoignez, à l'endroit de l'androgynat primitif, de connaissances profondes, ainsi que de préoccupations hautement philosophiques, celles-là mêmes qui étreignirent M. Champagne, lors de son retour du Plan de Grasse, et qui semblaient avoir bouleversé ses conceptions de naguère. Obéissant, l'un et l'autre, à cette orientation nouvelle, nous reprîmes l'étude du caput mortuum du premier oeuvre, que nous rejetions toujours comme des scories inutiles et sans valeur. Sans doute avions-nous tort en cela, puisque nombre de philosophes nous assurent que cette matière, d'aspect vulgaire et d'odeur forte, est la fleur de tous les métaux, le flos florum dont ils font tant de cas. Ils lui ont donné ce nom parce que, comme la fleur prépare le fruit et que le fruit est virtuellement dans la fleur, cette terre porte en elle l'embryon invisible d'un nouvel être minéral. La Tourbe nous en avertit en deux endroits différents: dans l'un, « Exinigamus dit: Sachez que toute nostre intention première est la veste ténébreuse vraye »; dans l'autre, « Theophilus dit: ... Sachez tous, fils de doctrine, que le secret de tout est une couverte ténébreuse, de laquelle les Philosophes ont tant de fois parlé. » De même, Avicenne enseigne que l'on doit « colliger nostre matière de la fiente, ordure et pourriture du Soleil et de la lune ». Quelques philosophes, pour caractériser l'impureté du magma d'où naît le lis hermétique, lui ont donné le nom de fumier. « Le sage sçait recognoistre nostre pierre jusque dans le fumier, assure le Cosmopolite, tandis que l'ignorant ne la sçauroit pas mesme trouver dans l'or. »

C'est un avertissement donné à l'artiste qui serait tenté, dans la séparation ou décomposition naturelle, de conserver le brillant, l'éclatant, le splendide, parce qu'il lui semble très pur, et de mépriser le fumier résiduel, ces fèces « ordes et infectes » au centre desquelles, cependant, gît et se dérobe le meilleur de ce qu'il cherche.

Je continue donc le travail du Grand Oeuvre dans cette direction que je ne doute pas que vous n'ayez imprimée aux expérimentations de M. Champagne. En conséquence, et surtout après la lecture d'Adam l'homme rouge, je suis fondé à croire que vous ayez vous-même obtenu au laboratoire cet hermès chimique, cette terre adamique qui est aussi Adam l'homme rouge. Ne dites-vous pas, pages 48 et 49, tout en établissant un saisissant parallèle entre les deux oeuvres, physico-humain et physico-chimique: « Pourquoi ces corps: soufre, sel et mercure? — Parce qu'ils sont typiques au possible. Le soufre, produit du feu de la terre; le mercure, l'eau des métaux, ou premier corps terrestre, et le sel, l'état stable naturellement le plus répandu. D'autre part, le soufre coagule le mercure et forme un sel noir et rouge. Jamais, il faut s'en souvenir, les philosophes rosicruciens n'ont pris les mots: soufre, sel et mercure,

Fig. 6.1. Letter from Eugène Canseliet to René Schwaller de Lubicz. The letter is translated in appendix F.

pour autre chose que pour des symboles de la trinité. Mais cela <u>la mentalité</u> <u>intellectualisée</u> <u>de la science</u> de nos jours ne peut presque pas le comprendre."

« Il y a un principe qui agit, un principe qui reçoit, et les deux forment par mutuel amour, — (attraction et répulsion successives de la génération), — le sel parfait qui est Trois en Un, Dieu dans la trinité, appelé dans l'œuvre matérielle des philosophes : la pierre philosophale. Le mot « pierre » signifie ici symboliquement la forme parfaite, la plus dure, la plus matérielle, la plus formelle ; et le qualificatif « philosophale » signifie qu'elle est à entendre dans le sens de la connaissance ésotérique... »

Tout ce passage, à mon sens, constitue une révélation qui n'est pas de moindre importance.

Également, page 89, voici un bien grand secret dans un petit alinéa :

« Quant à la femme, elle garde en elle le souvenir de la déchéance d'homme en femme. Elle ne peut devenir homme qu'en se <u>confondant</u> avec lui. Alors les deux ne seront plus deux, mais un <u>corps</u> animé. »

Ne se peut-il pas que M. Champagne ait fait preuve encore, à l'égard de cette partie matérielle y de vos travaux, d'une absence de mémoire aussi incompréhensible que surprenante sinon d'une discrétion hors de propos et d'une réserve peut-être excessive. Quoi qu'il en soit, je ne parviens pas à chasser l'impression douloureuse qu'ont laissé en moi, des événements imprévus, des faits insoupçonnés qui se sont produits à la fin de sa vie, puis après sa mort, et qui ont donné lieu à des scènes atroces, dont je n'aurais trop dire qu'elles eussent été plus écœurantes que pénibles. Il subsistait, d'ailleurs, depuis longtemps, l'ascendant déplorable, insensiblement acquis sur lui par une femme, et que les êtres bornés exercent, hélas ! trop souvent, sur les esprits supérieurs.

Mais tout cela n'est rien et n'offre d'autre intérêt que celui, négligeable en soi, qu'on peut attacher aux choses factices de ce monde. Tout autre est la valeur que je donne à la réponse que vous croirez bon de m'adresser, afin de m'éclairer, dans la mesure où vous jugerez <u>utile</u> de le faire, sur le point capital du grand ouvrage.

Je vous prie d'agréer, Monsieur, mes meilleures salutations.

*Canseliet*

Eugène Canseliet
18 Quai des Célestins
Paris — 4e

and truly the disciple of Champagne and that he held him in great esteem, to the point of working with him for seven years, from 1925 to 1932.

Jean-Julien Champagne had always kept secret his meetings with René Schwaller. He had revealed nothing of his long collaboration with Schwaller or of their experiments in the laboratory. Eugène Canseliet knew simply that in the last few years of Champagne's life, ties between the two men had become closer. We could say that he suspected the importance of their collaboration. As he wrote to Schwaller, "You demonstrate profound knowledge at the juncture of the primitive androgynous state, as well as highly philosophical concerns—in fact the same as those that gripped Mr. Champagne upon his return from Plan-de-Grasse and which seemed to overturn his former notions . . ."

Eugène Canseliet was certainly not party to the work carried out by Pierre Dujols and Julien Champagne on the notes that were to give birth to *Le Mystères des Cathédrales* any more than he was aware of the association of Dujols and Champagne in the preparation of the future *Demeures Philosophales*.* He was also unaware of the laboratory work on the blues and reds of Chartres's stained glass. Gaston Devaux, J.-J. Champagne's brother-in-law, who acted as a forwarding address for Champagne, further deepened the mystery. After the death of the alchemist in 1932, Eugène Canseliet continued to maintain connections with the Devaux family, visiting them in the département of the Somme, and subsequently invited the family to his home.

---

*"I am obliged here to make a brief parenthetical remark in order to warn the reader against the intellectual deception of those who claim to be Frères d'Héliopolis (Brothers of Heliopolis) or who claim the existence of Fulcanelli. On this subject, thanks to Jacques Bergier, Lucien Carny, Jean Haab, and Robert Ambelain, I am in possession of indications that allow us to state without reservation: 'Fulcanelli no more existed than did the Marquis de B—.' All that is part of a modern, now-classic, obfuscation, which takes the reader to be an idiot or someone quite gullible." Jean-Luc Chaumeil, *Le Trésor des Templiers* (Paris: Connaissance de l'Étrange, Henri Veyrier, 1984), 223.

See also what Paul de Saint-Hilaire has written in his *Atlas du Mystère* (Luxembourg: RTL Éditions, 1985), 211: "These two works have certainly been at the basis of a renewing of alchemy. However, based on elements that had been assembled by a scholar who knew his material perfectly well, the text seems to have been rewritten by a third party and artificially stuffed with obscure facts drawn from the jumble of certain grimoires. To be read with caution and discernment."

This legendary history detracts neither from the interest the protagonists have for the science of the philosophers nor from their contribution to the understanding of the texts of the ancients. We are simply reminded of the article of Giovanni Sciuto that appeared in the journal *L'Autre Monde,* special issue on alchemy (1987), which attempts to prove that Nicolas Flamel was not an adept and that "having entered into legend, he is in the process of getting himself out of it." Indeed, according to the historian of science Robert Halleux, from Belgium, a specialist in the history of alchemy, Nicolas Flamel certainly existed and was wealthy enough to perform charitable works, but his personality as an adept was established a century later in the 1700s* in order to give a new appeal to this science, which was in decline. In this regard it was an anonymous alchemical author who was to have created the legend.

As for the book called *Livre des lavures,* attributed to Flamel, its style is not that of the fourteenth century but rather that of the time of the Renaissance. History repeats itself.

## Versions of the Myth

We are now going to broach a few points in the assertions of Eugène Canseliet that have seemed suspicious and which have to do with the extraordinary story of the survival of Fulcanelli as an adept in a "parallel" world, through recountings that took place over many years.

In 1953, in his book *L'Occultisme à Paris,* Pierre Geyraud (alias Abbé Guyades, vicar of Saint-Séverin) narrates that in 1936, during a banquet attended by a glittering array of society figures on the occasion of the feast of the sun and the festival of lights of St. John, Eugène Canseliet replied to a question of Mr. Rosny concerning the identity of Fulcanelli:

> . . . Fulcanelli is the pseudonym of [an] individual about whom, out of respect for the hermetic rule of silence, I cannot speak in any other way. This Fulcanelli *is still alive.* He is mandated by the White

---

*However, it should be pointed out that the oldest references to the alchemical activities of Nicolas Flamel appear about fifty years after his death.

Brotherhood to assist in the evolution of humanity. This is a true Rosy-Cross. He is sometimes in Brazil, sometimes in Argentina, wandering through the world in the manner of the Rosy-Cross of olden times. Right now he is in the south of France. He is a master with amazing powers."[1]

This story highlights the belief of Canseliet in the alchemical mythology: the mandated adept, longevity, powers, and so on.

In 1972, in the *Charivari* devoted to alchemy, there appears the "Seville Story" from the pen of François Jacquemart:

In *1952,* a female acquaintance of Eugène Canseliet came to Canseliet's home and asked him to follow her without specifying the destination, but letting him know that it was a matter of some importance. The trip came to an end not far from Seville, at a rambling estate where a terrace and a double set of stairs led to a stately home. Upon his arrival, Fulcanelli (remember that he was born in 1840) was there and asked Canseliet: "Do you recognize me?" Eugène Canseliet assented. The two men engaged in a brief exchange. For the remainder of the stay, they met only for short moments. Eugène Canseliet was working in what he heard called "the small laboratory." Early one morning, in one of the walkways of the park after one of the long nights of labors in which he had been compelled to engage, he saw a strange scene: *a young queen wearing the Golden Fleece was moving forward,* followed by a duenna. Seeing him, she nodded. On another occasion, he came upon two children, a little boy and a little girl, playing with two rabbits and a pony. From their clothing and their appearance they seemed to have stepped out of a Velázquez painting. On these two occasions, Eugène Canseliet had the intuition of a humanity that was not living on the same plane as ours, a society beyond time . . .

In his 1969 book, *Invitation au château de l'étrange—témoignages inédits* (Invitation to the Chateau of the Strange—Unpublished Accounts), Claude Seignolle recounts a story that took place in 1966 and in which the central figure is Eugène Canseliet. There is no mention of Fulcanelli in this account, nor of Seville, but only of a strange family who fascinated Canseliet for their alchemical knowledge and the impression they gave of living as though "stuck in the seventeenth century."[2]

*Fig. 6.2. Eugène Canseliet. Photograph taken by Guy Béatrice and kindly provided by Mrs. Guy Béatrice*

## The Trip to Castille

In revealing this confidential adventure, I am going to betray the trust of a friend and his two daughters with whom I have for a long time established a substantial exchange of affection. [He is] a simple man, modest and, it goes without saying, sincere. His knowledge is vast and authentic. Of course, I will remain silent as to his name, famous and respected as he is in esoteric circles, but I bow in advance before his reproach, in case these lines should fall before his eyes.

Every day he receives a ministerial volume of post and engages in fascinating exchanges of correspondence, among them with a wealthy Spanish family who are said to be withdrawn from time and who write in a marvelously textured antique French—a joy for my friend, who readily uses the imperfect subjunctive, even with his grocer.

Two or three years ago, this Spanish family sent him a plane ticket to Madrid, inviting him to spend a few days with them so they would come to know him better, while, for their part, they would endeavor to learn more from him about his specialty— which seemed impossible! The adventure was tempting. My friend, although not very inclined to accept such an invitation, felt that he would make interesting discoveries, for the tone and context of the letters he had received over the years were remarkable as much for their subtle observations as for the riches they contained.

He took the plane. At the Madrid airport an old Spanish woman was waiting for him with a chauffeur, who was more like a coachman than an automobile driver, decked out in antique style and looking as though he might well be found in the corner of a Goya painting. No one else was there to greet him, and the driver was very tight-lipped. Allowing himself to be driven away, my friend settled into a customary smiling contemplation. They traversed a long road to arrive, near dusk, at the wrought-iron gate of a park enclosed by a high wall. But they had not yet arrived at the destination: A winding, rocky road led them in one direction and then another, as if it were about to lose itself. . . . Finally they stopped at a broad terrace. The driver stopped the motor, got out, and, taking my friend's suitcase, invited him to follow. A walkway led them away. They walked for a long time and came to a large old dwelling, low-set but majestic.

In coming into the house, my friend noticed that there was no electricity. Not one lightbulb. Here only candles were used for lighting. Was this done in his honor, to recall the Spain of yesteryear, or was it an everyday occurrence? His hosts were there, wearing traditional vestments, which, far from finding grotesque, he enjoyed immensely. "Finally," he thought, "here are people who know how to remove themselves from this century where the fashions are so changeable and sometimes so daring. Here, all the women are in long dresses, velvet or brocade, and the men in a kind of doublet with stockings and buckled shoes."

Everyone crowded around the master come from afar and they feted him royally (I am putting myself for a moment in the place of this delightful man when he hears a smooth old French spoken by the old Castilian).

The welcoming meal had the same yesteryear flavor—the dishes as well as the service. As for the conversation, it was appropriately astounding. My friend quickly noticed, as he had in their letters, that his hosts, although they might have been hesitant about present-day alchemy, had, on the contrary, very profound knowledge of ancient alchemy, which they spoke of naturally, as if it was something that they made use of every day. This was true to such an extent that my friend—he who knows all knowledge—learned, with amazement, of the existence of unknown books and the wording of forgotten formulas, finding in these people the lost strength of ancient alchemy.

Who then were these individuals living in 1966 but having not ventured past the life of the seventeenth century? He was very careful not to ask them. Besides, had he not seen others like this in his life as a magician?

His sojourn there lasted a week, and not only did he learn a great deal, but he underwent a beneficial rest cure. He saw planes pass by overhead but did not hear the slightest hum, and on the nearby road, cars came and went in silence as if the present moment was nothing more than a vision of the mind. Around him there were no other sounds except those of an affable and peaceful family who each day seemed tirelessly to resume their patient gestures and, devoid of any agitation, to speak of a life that had no end.

In *1978,* Robert Amadou's *Feu du Soleil* was published. In it there is this conversation with Eugène Canseliet:

It was near Seville. I was walking like a king. Everything I needed was there, but I always came back to my lodging, and I left again early in the morning. In the garden there were apples and lemons. A freshwater stream flowed nearby. It was magnificent!

Now I did not expect to meet Fulcanelli, with my suspenders tumbling down my trousers.

When he saw me, he addressed me familiarly, as he was accustomed to do: "So, do you recognize me?"

And on the previous page: "He is no longer there; he is on the earth, but it is a terrestrial paradise. What is he doing now? I saw nothing. I saw him when I arrived, when he greeted me wearing a suit."

Finally: "And in the manor where I saw Fulcanelli, there were contemporaries of Philip II. Right away, I understood nothing. It was not forbidden to look out the windows, and I saw a very beautiful staircase with a number of landings, and children playing. . . . There were also many young women who looked as if they had stepped out of a Velázquez painting, with the collar of the Golden Fleece."[3]

*In 1979,* in the meeting between Jacques Pradel and Eugène Canseliet on France-Inter, the same story turns up again, but the apparent age of Fulcanelli is specified: from his looks, about fifty, although he should have been 113. "That year, a car stopped in front of the house of Eugène Canseliet near Beauvais. In this car, there was an emissary from Fulcanelli. Someone showed Eugène Canseliet papers that proved Fulcanelli was alive. Eugène Canseliet was going to find himself in Spain, in a mysterious chateau near Seville, he thinks. . . . There are people on the earth who are living on a different plane than ours, that is certain."

Finally, in *The Fulcanelli Phenomenon,* by Kenneth Rayner Johnson, Canseliet recounts that one morning, in his bedroom of the little tower that he was occupying, he moved near to the window and saw a group of three women who seemed to be dressed in the style of the sixteenth century. He was about to go back to his room when one of the women turned toward him and began to laugh. He was stunned, for the face of the "woman" who was laughing as she looked at him was that of *Fulcanelli.*[4]

In this book, the voyage to Spain is dated 1954, in contrast to what Eugène Canseliet states in *Feu du Soleil,* which gives the date as 1952.

Also according to Rayner Johnson, someone had been able to see in Eugène Canseliet's passport an entry visa to Spanish territory for the year 1954.

After hearing these accounts, we can say that it is possible that Eugène Canseliet is relating a paranormal experience. This may remind the reader of the story of the "Fantômes de Trianon,"[5] in which two Englishwomen visited Versailles at the beginning of the twentieth century and found themselves plunged into the middle of the eighteenth century. They met courtesans who spoke to them and were able even to see Marie-Antoinette.

These two, Miss Moberly and Miss Jourdain, were apparently trustworthy, and their story never varied. It is known that there is an emotional charge underlying a paranormal experience and that retelling such an experience can be stabilizing.

The 1957 edition of *Le Mystère des Cathédrales* was expanded to include a chapter attributed to Fulcanelli that has led to much commentary: "The Cyclic Cross of Hendaye."

Mr. Canseliet makes no mention of the article that appeared in 1936 in *Consolation,* the journal directed by Maryse Choisy (see figs. 6.3, 6.4, 6.5) and signed Jules Boucher (J. B.). In this article we find virtually all theories about the famous inscription OCRUXAVES PESUNIC A.

Nous avons trouvé à Hendaye cette croix dont le symbolisme est vraiment curieux.

Elle s'élève sur trois marches et la base est ornée sur chacune de ses faces :

Sur la face Ouest, le Soleil ; sur la face Est, une Étoile à huit pointes ; sur la face Sud, quatre A et sur la face Nord, la Lune.

La croix elle-même porte sur la face Ouest cette inscription : **O Crux Ave Spes Unica**; et derrière les quatre lettres I.N.R.I. La branche supérieure est ornée de l'X ou croix de Saint-André.

Notons encore que la branche horizontale est orientée du nord au sud, comme l'aiguille aimantée d'une boussole.

### L'inscription
### « O Crux Ave S pes Unic a »

Ce qui attire tout d'abord notre attention, c'est que le mot « **Spes** » est volontairement séparé en deux parties : **S** et **Pes**. Il y a là une intention bien nette. L'artiste qui a sculpté cette inscription n'a certainement pas voulu faire ressortir le mot **Pes**, mot qui signifie **Pied**. Et, la lettre finale, l'**A** de **Unica** est éloignée elle aussi.

Ainsi l'auteur nous montre que ce n'est pas par manque de place qu'il a placé la lettre **S** initiale de **Spes** dans la ligne supérieure.

Il s'agit donc ici d'une phrase cabalistique qu'il faut lire **phonétiquement** en permutant les voyelles selon les principes des Initiés du Moyen Âge.

Et cette phrase, si nous savons la lire, nous donnera la clef du monument tout entier.

Voici le sens le plus simple que nous pouvons exprimer :

**O Croix Have Espace Unique** et la croix étant le symbole de la mort puisque c'est elle que l'on place sur tous les tombeaux, nous lisons : **O Mort hâve espace unique.**

Cette croix nous indique alors qu'elle se rapporte au Cycle de l'existence et à la fin du monde. Elle montre aux Initiés quelles seront les parties du monde qui seront atteintes et aussi où se trouvera le salut.

C'est le Feu qui doit provoquer la fin de notre cycle; aussi, au verso de cette inscription, nous lisons : I.N.R.I., **Ignis Naturæ Renovatur Integra**, le Feu de la Nature renouvelle tout entièrement.

### Le Soleil dévorant

Immédiatement au-dessous de cette inscription, nous trouvons l'image du « Soleil dévorant ». L'expression de cette figure est frappante.

---

Ce soleil possède 16 rayons. Or, dans le tarot, la seizième lame est la **Maison-Dieu**, la ruine, la catastrophe. D'ailleurs, le chiffre égale $1 + 6$, c'est-à-dire 7. Et nous savons que 7 c'est la faux, c'est la Mort.

Cette face regarde l'Ouest. C'est donc l'Occident qui sera détruit.

Ce Soleil, entouré de quatre étoiles, nous dit que seule la volonté agissante peut éviter le cataclysme.

### L'Étoile

C'est une étoile qui est sculptée sur la face Est. Une étoile toute simple, sans ornements superflus. Cette étoile, c'est l'espérance, c'est le salut. Le Salut est à l'Orient.

Cette étoile possède huit rayons. Huit, c'est le chiffre de la Justice. Les justes, les sages, les initiés reconnaîtront ici leur Étoile.

### La Lune

Au nord, figure la Lune. La lune, c'est l'intuition et l'inspiration. C'est aussi la Connaissance. C'est pourquoi l'artiste a sculpté une œil de face, comme dans les figurations égyptiennes. On sait que les Égyptiens ne représentaient jamais l'œil de profil. Cet œil nous indique aussi la vision dans l'obscurité, c'est-à-dire la connaissance secrète.

### Les Quatre A

Enfin, au sud, nous trouvons les **Quatre A**. C'est-à-dire les quatre âges.

La division des âges la plus généralement admise est celle qu'a suivie Ovide et qui renferme quatre périodes :

**L'Age d'Or, l'Age d'Argent, l'Age d'Airain et l'Age de Fer.**

« Les hommes, dans l'Age d'Or, spontanément et sans lois gardaient la bonne foi et la justice; le châtiment et la crainte étaient ignorés. La trompette, le clairon, le casque, l'épée, n'existaient pas encore, et, sans l'appui des armées, les peuples, au sein de la sécurité, coulaient d'heureux loisirs. La terre aussi, sans être déchirée par la charrue, prodiguait d'elle-même tous les biens.

Alors régnait un printemps éternel, alors serpentaient les fleuves de lait et de nectar; et de l'yeuse toujours verte distillait les rayons dorés du miel.

Avec l'Age d'Argent, viennent l'hiver, l'été, l'automne inégal et un printemps resserré dans d'étroites limites. Alors, pour la première fois, les hommes pénètrent sous l'abri d'une demeure; ils eurent pour maison les antres, un toit formé d'épaisses broussailles ou de branchages entrecroisés; alors pour la première fois, les semences de Cérès furent confiées à de longs sillons, et les jeunes taureaux gémirent sous le poids du joug.

A ces deux âges, succède l'Age d'Airain : l'homme plus féroce est plus prompt à prendre les armes qui sèment l'effroi : il s'abstient cependant du crime.

Le dernier est l'Age de Fer. A l'instant, tous les crimes se font jour; la pudeur, la vérité, la bonne foi, prennent la fuite; à leur place succèdent la ruse, l'artifice, la trahison, la violence et la coupable soif de posséder. Les arbres, après avoir longtemps séjourné sur la cime des monts, transformés en vaisseaux, bravent les flots inconnus. La terre avait été jusque-là commune à tous, comme l'air et la lumière; alors le laboureur, défiant, entoure son champ d'une limite. On ne se contente plus de demander à la terre féconde les moissons et les aliments nécessaires; on descend jusque dans ses entrailles, et les richesses qu'elle y tenait cachées près des ténèbres du Styx, tirées à la lumière, donnent

---

l'éveil à tous les maux. Bientôt se montre le fer, si nuisible, l'or plus nuisible encore, la guerre qui les prend l'un et l'autre pour instrument, et dont la main rougie dans le sang secoue des armes bruyantes. On vit de rapines. »

Telle est la peinture que l'auteur des **Métamorphoses** nous a laissée de la vie primitive de l'humanité. C'est par allusion à cette description que nous employons les expressions d'**Age d'Or et de Fer** pour désigner un temps heureux et une période de crimes et de calamités. Mais la mythologie gréco-romaine n'est pas la seule qui nous offre, sous cette apparence symbolique, l'histoire d'un cycle de l'humanité. Cette tradition des quatre âges se retrouve avec quelques différences de forme, chez la plupart des peuples de l'antiquité, en Égypte et dans l'Inde. Elle est, par exemple, fort explicitement développée dans la cosmogonie de Manou. Au reste, la distinction des deux âges extrêmes, l'Age d'Or et l'Age de Fer, est ici le fait fondamental. Or, cette tradition est une croyance universelle qu'on a retrouvée chez tous les peuples, à tous les états de barbarie et de civilisation. Il en résulte nécessairement que cette tradition a un fondement historique réel, qu'elle repose sur un fait qui, malgré les altérations diverses qu'il a

**SUD**

subies en se transformant de génération en génération, a toujours son caractère essentiel.

○ ○ ○

La branche supérieure de la croix est ornée d'une croix de Saint-André. Écoutons ce que nous dit **Fulcanelli**, dans les **Demeures philosophales** :

« Les Bohémiens utilisent la croix ou l'X comme signe de reconnaissance. Guidés par ce graphique tracé sur un arbre ou sur quelque mur, ils campent toujours exactement à la place qu'occupaient leurs prédécesseurs, auprès du symbole sacré qu'ils nomment : **Patria**. On pourrait croire ce mot d'origine latine et le rapporter à cette maxime : **Patria est ubicumque est bene**, partout où l'on est bien, là est la patrie; mais c'est d'un mot grec, **Patria**, que se réclame leur emblème, avec le sens de **famille, race, tribu**. La croix des romanichels ou gipsies indique donc, nettement, le lieu du refuge attribué à la tribu. Il est singulier, d'ailleurs, que presque toutes les significations révélées par le signe du X ont une valeur transcendante ou mystérieuse.

*Fig. 6.3. The article in* Consolation *by Jules Boucher on the cyclic cross at Hendaye*

**ndaye**

OUEST

OUEST

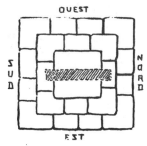

SUD

NORD

EST

EST

X c'est, en algèbre, la ou les quantités inconnues; c'est aussi le problème à résoudre, la solution à découvrir. »

NORD

Cette croix, signée par l'X, nous montre qu'il s'agit là d'une sorte de rébus. Et l'artiste a multiplié les figures afin que son emblème soit parlant.

Les monuments religieux sont ceux qui sont le plus respectés, aussi en donant cette forme à ce jalon était-il sûr de sa conservation.

Nous ne terminerons pas sans indiquer aux « cabalistes » qu'en scrutant attentivement, avec les yeux de l'esprit, l'inscription « **O Crux Ave Spes Unica**, telle qu'elle se trouve inscrite sur notre croix, ils trouveront très exactement et sans erreur possible l'indication précise du point du globe qui ne sera pas touché par la prochaine catastrophe, par le prochain **bouleversement**.

Qu'on prenne garde que ce mot « bouleversement » signifie renversement de la boule, renversement de la sphère terrestre. C'est-à-dire que le pôle nord deviendra le pôle sud et inversement quand le Soleil dévorant (se reporter à notre article sur le Soleil Noir), arrivé au point culminant de sa course, marchera en sens inverse, tout en gardant le même sens de rotation.

Nous ne pouvons exposer ici publiquement les traditions secrètes; mais ces doctrines seront données aux membres de l'A.R.O.T. qui en seront jugés dignes. L'A.R.O.T. (Association pour la Révolution de l'Occultisme Traditionnel) est, nous l'avons déjà dit, un groupement véritablement initiatique.

o o o

Nous devons à l'aimable obligeance de M. Lemoine, peintre de grand talent, les documents qui illustrent cet article. Qu'il veuille bien trouver ici l'expression de notre reconnaissance.

Nous avions signalé à M. Lemoine l'existence de cette croix et nous lui avions demandé de nous rapporter soit des croquis, soit des photographies et nous ne savions pas où cette croix se trouvait exactement. Ici se place une anecdote que nous voulons rapporter :

M. Lemoine demanda à plusieurs personnes si elles connaissaient une croix répondant à la description que je lui avais donnée et il obtint constamment des réponses négatives. Avisant un prêtre qui passait, il lui posa la même question. Cet excellent abbé lui répondit que toutes les croix répondaient à la description qu'il donnait et ajouta qu'il croyait qu'il n'y en avait qu'à Hendaye. Voici le dialogue tel qu'il nous fut transmis :

— Mais pourquoi recherchez-vous cela ?

— C'est pour un de mes amis de Paris qui s'occupe d'Archéologie.

— Mais pourquoi est-ce faire ? Dans quel but ?

— Je vous l'ai dit. Uniquement archéologique.

— Cette personne doit s'occuper d'autres choses que d'Archéologie.

Et le bon abbé s'éloigna.

Alors, notre ami erra dans la ville, bien décidé à découvrir notre petit monument. Il le trouva, en effet, et s'installa pour prendre photographies et croquis. A ce moment, le prêtre passa et lui lança, nous dit-il, un furieux regard.

Pourquoi toujours et partout cette volonté d'obscurantisme. Est-ce une consigne, un mot d'ordre ?

La croix d'Hendaye subira sans doute prochainement le sort de bien d'autres. On la détruira sous un prétexte quelconque et on la remplacera par une grotesque croix de fer sans signification aucune.

Il est juste de reconnaître que le symbolisme de la Croix d'Hendaye ne présente pas un sens religieux bien net, et ceci a dû et doit gêner considérablement MM. les apôtres de la Foi.

*Fig. 6.4. One of the sides of the base of the cyclic cross at Hendaye.*
*Photograph by José Fuentes*

*Fig. 6.5. The cyclic cross at Hendaye*

Robert Ambelain entrusted us with the rather shocking unfolding of this discovery. As it happened, on vacation with his lady friend in Hendaye, the painter Lemoine took a photograph of the monument, seeing in it a "teaching." He submitted a print of it to Maryse Choisy, who, on the lookout for articles for her weekly, asked Jules Boucher to write something about this "esoteric" cross. Boucher told Robert Ambelain that he was not much interested in the subject but didn't know how to get out of doing it. He did his best and the article appeared in 1936.

As for the sundial of Holyrood (fig. 6.6), which was the subject of a chapter in *Les Demeures Philosophales,* some are quick to see it as proof that Fulcanelli belonged to an aristocratic milieu. Today it is not possible to gain access to this monument, which is found in the private gardens of the royal family of England.

It seems clear that René Schwaller, who was a member of the Theosophical Society, communicated a drawing or a photograph like this to Jean-Julien Champagne with the assistance of the theosophist Lady Caithness.

In her mansion on the avenue Wagram, Lady Caithness gathered the whole esoteric milieu of her time. She had been behind the founding of the Gnostic Church and was the representative in France of the Theosophical Society. Her husband was Lord James Barogill, the fourteenth count of Caithness, who was head of the Sinclair clan. He was buried in the former royal chapel of Mary Stuart at Holyrood.

Lady Caithness was very much a part of fashionable English society and was obsessively devoted to Mary Stuart, believing herself to be Mary's reincarnation, for in the abbey of Holyrood she had had an experience with the dead queen.

In volume 2 of *Les Demeures Philosophales,* the chapter "Paradoxe du progrès illimité des sciences" (Paradox of the Unlimited Progress of Science, missing from the first edition) is about the incineration of the planet. To support his ideas about this, the author mentions a church at Melle, in the département of Deux-Sèvres, the porch of which is

MARY QUEEN OF SCOTS' SUN-DIAL,
*in the Garden of Holyrood Palace.*

Fig. 6.6. The Holyrood sundial

ornamented with an equestrian statue referred to as the Horseman of the Apocalypse.*

Those who are curious and want to admire this sculpture can go to this charming town, where they would first of all find that the horseman is not in the entrance of the church of Saint-Pierre but instead in the church of Saint-Hilaire.

Next they would notice that this handsome figure is over the side door of the church's *north* side and not its *south* side, as the author contends. Yet the text bases the point of its hypothesis concerning the mysterious horseman on just this southerly orientation: "It is a serious and noble statue that, in the gallery of a semicircular arch of the church of Saint-Pierre, rears up over the southern entrance, always subjected to the radiance of the sun due to this orientation."

We shall finish with the book by Atorène, *Le Laboratoire alchimique,* in which there is mention of the rue Dieudé in Marseilles, where Fulcanelli is supposed to have stayed in 1915. Figure 6.7 (pages 119–120) shows the list of those who lived on the rue Dieudé. As it turns out, the archivist Isabelle Bonnot looked for evidence of a possible trip of Eugène Canseliet to the Fine Arts Museum of Marseilles and found nothing.

*According to the most accepted opinion on the twelfth century, this statue, which is found rather frequently at the entrance of churches in Poitou, represents the emperor Constantine driving out paganism. See Émile Mâle, *L'Art religieux du XIIe siècle en France* (Religious Art in Twelfth-Century France).

*Fig. 6.7. Address directory by street for Marseilles, dating from 1915. All the inhabitants of the rue Dieudé are listed.*

**Pensionnat Dieudé. H. Prat (Mme)**
direct.
**J.** Bonnet entrepreneur de manu-
tention·
Dominique Orus, acconier.
N. Zérati, commerçant·
**Eug. Rousset.**
A. Perrin·
Louis Julien·
Turin. P. (Vve), propriét
Beillon. Jean. ✚.
Pignon frères. tapissiers.
Carlevan, employé·
*R. Fongate* 22.
Ch· Berrut·
B. Foa (Mme), rentière·
Georges Aicard·
Roux (de), Henry·
Roux (de), Paul. art. peintre.
Turcat (Vve), rentière·
R. ux (de) Michel (Mme)·
Rocca (l'abbé)·
*Cours Lieutaud* 64.
Polis-Legrand (Mme)·
Henri Odet. ébéniste.
E. Pailloux, organiste·
Louis Richard·
J. Sponti·
Elie Monnet·
Marius Béraud, entrepreneur·
Fé ix Pontié. tailleur·
*R. Fongate* 16.

**Dominicaines** (rue des), de la rue
d'Aix 20 a, au boul. d'Athènes 31.
(343 m. 95 de long.)
Carré G. 9.

Circonscription électorale : 3me. — Justice de
paix : 3me cant. (boul. des Dames 27). —
Police : 2me arrondissem. (rue Tapis-Vert
17). — Percept : 3me arrond. ( r. Clapier, 43)
— Paroisse : S aint-Théodore.

1 *R. d'Aix* 20.
Église Saint-Théodore·
Antonin Bossy, auteur lyrique.
2 *R. d'Aix* 2.
Lard ayret (Vve), teinturerie.
Léon Chazvie. employé.
Pierre Durand, propriétaire.
G Nakamoura (Mme)·
François Novel, 22. tailleur.
3 Emile Bourguet. droguiste.
4 F. Plat·
Victor Sause,
J. Chabaud, boucher.
Guillaume Mallaroni. employé·
Antoine Levet, employé.
5 *R. de l'Etoile* 4.
L. Bernard. fab. de casquettes.
Eugène Aillaud. vins·
6 F. Fuzigiando. voyag. de comm·
R. Piccardi, tissus.
Gabrielle Decome (Mme)·
Quinte Biamonti·
Ch. Barnouin. beurres et fromages.
J. Olive (Vve). dorure sur cuir et
soie.
7 Michel, T., bonneterie·
Bachmann, employé·
Gabriel Valette.
H. Girard. employé.
A. Lespinasse. principal clerc
d'avoué.
Eugène Imbert.
Henri Tourrettes. docteur en mé-
decine.
Albert Bosse (Mme), corsets.
Albert Bosse. employé·
8 H. Lajard (le chanoine)·
F. Cohne. professeur de piano et
de flûte.
Jérôme Barral·
8 et 10 Ernest Chazottes. lingerie.
9 Vernis et Rolland. drogueries.
G. Pellegrin. employé.
M. Pellegrin. ajusteur-mécanicien
M. Pellegrin. institutrice·
P. Pellegrin, employé.
*R. des Petites-Maries* 1.
10 Marius Araud, coiffeur.
Camille Roman.
11 *R. des Petites-Maries* 2.
Marius Troin. rentier·
Troin (Mme), rentière.
Ch. Astarito, épicier.
12 D. Romano. fabric. bijoutier.
Cinéma St-Théodore.
13 ......................
14 Joseph Payan.
A. Sarlin.
Pelloquin. Henri·

14 P. Mistral (l'abbé). curé de Saint-
Théodore.
Louis Roux.
15 J. Génon, agent de publicité.
M. Estachy. plomberie.
Sauze-Romain. fabrique de cou-
ronnes mortuaires.
G. Arnoux·
16 J. Drujon. meublé·
L. Drujon. bar.
17 P. Monges, meublé·
*R. du Baignoir* 18.
18 Jérôme Colombani, mercerie.
C. Giraud (Vve)·
Eyraud (Mme)·
19 *R. du Baignoir* 41.
Morel (Vve), laiterie-crémerie.
Julie Rosso (Mme), vins et huiles.
Garrik (Vve), meublé·
20 Louis Rossi, peinture, vitrerie.
Mortier. S. (Dlle). modiste·
Paul Loniewski. employé.
Rollino (Mme), rentière·
21 Rose Gilles (Dlle), repasseuse et
meublé
22 Gaspard Mauras, employé.
Léouffre. (Vve)·
23 T. Marcellin. beurres et fromages.
T. Riou, chapelier.
Antoinette Pulella (Dlle), rentière·
24 A. Magallon, boucherie·
M. Riquel (Vve), rentière.
J. Riquet, rentier·
25 Chiappone (Vve). meublé·
Albrand (Dlle). repasseuse.
26 A. Bermond. bar et épicerie.
A. Journiac. mécanicien à bord.
Fière (Vve).
*Rue du Baignoir*. 39.
27 Pauget, tabletier·
Marius Panisse, meublé.
28 *R. du Baignoir* 16.
B. Dalmas. meublé.
29 J. Putto. bois et charbons.
30 Touzé (Mme). professeur de piano
J. Ollivier (Dlle), rentière·
A. Beaussan (Vve). rentière·
31 Marius Isnard, meublé.
32 A. Brun. comptable.
E. Alamel, voyageur de commer.
E. Ripert. fabric-bijontier.
33 Léon Jean, boulangerie.
*Rue de la Fare* 7.
34 Raymond de Roux.
Raoul d'Esclapon (de). R.
Ravel d'Esclapon (de) E.
35 *R. de la Fare* 8.
Grand (Dlles), employées.
F. Canagnier. représentant.
36 A. Telesfer. meublé
37 R. Barnabe. meublé.
38 J. B. Vottero. herboriste.
C. Cardon (Vve)·
Rambert. A. (Dlle) employée.
Vottero (Vve)·
V. Vottero. fils.
39 Jean Revel. meublé.
*Rue Longue-des-Capucins* 63.
40 *R. de la Fare* 10.
B. Chiappone (Vve), meublé·
41 *R. Longue-des-Capucins* 66
A. Perrier. propriétaire.
Cros (Mme), primeurs.
Humbert Vallet, représentant.
A. Mestrallet. voyag. de commerce
E. Bennet, représentant.
42 Gabriel Garronite, verreries·
*R. Longue-des-Capucins* 61.
43 Procure de la Société des Missions
Africaines.
S Desribes (l'abbé). ✚. ✚.
C. Lissner·
44 *R. Longue-des-Capucins* 64.
E. Gounin. cond. des P. et C. en ret,
M. Casanova (Vve)·
J. Décanis (Dlle), institution de
demoiselles
45 Marius Aynaud, empl. au P.-L.-M.
Adrien Rolland, employé P.-L.-M.
46 ......................
47 Joseph Pensa. Q A., courtier
J. Rolland. employé P.-L.-M.
J.-B. Jeanselme. bijoutier·
Charles Delage. bijoutier·
48 J. Willis (Mme). institution de demoiselles
49 Sendrané et Gumchian. grains et
légumes secs·
Edouard Gardair. négociant.
Marius Gasquet·
50 Hôtel des chambres syndicales pa-
tronales·

50 Fédération des syndicats commer-
ciaux. industriels et agricoles
des Bouches-du-Rhône.
Union syndicale des commerçants
en vins de l'arrond. de Marseille·
Syndicat des magasiniers march.
de beurres et fromages.
Syndicat des épiciers de l'arrondis-
sement de Marseille.
Syndicat des patrons coiffeurs.
Syndicat des Forains·
Chambre syndicale des débitants
de boissons.
Bouchers-charcutiers (patrons).
Syndicat des bouchers-charcutiers
(magasiniers).
Syndicat de l'épicerie de Marseille
et du département.
Syndicat de l'alimentation mar-
seillaise
Office de placement des patrons
coiffeurs.
Syndicat de Défense des Intérêts
des Commerçants magasiniers·
Fédération des laitiers de Mar-
seille.
Association corporative des mar-
chands de lapins et volailles
Le Courrier du Commerce (journ.)
Le Moniteur de la Boulangerie
(journal).
Le Journal de la Boucherie.
Louis Godard. publiciste.
Syndicat des Gérants de Débits de
tabacs des B.-du-Rh.
*Le Gérant* (journal).
Syndicat des Confiseurs, Pâtissiers
et Chocolatiers·
Syndicat des Pâtissiers détaillants.
Fédération des Syndicats com mer-
ciaux. industriels et agrico es.
Syndicat des bouchers-charcutiers
de Marseille.
51 Société des Etablissements Léon
Panlet.
*R. de l'Eclipse* 1.
55 *R. de l'Eclipse* 2.
Ecole communale maternelle.
Françoise Boudinaud, directrice·
Eug. Boudinaud, employé.
D. Boudinaud employé·
Louise Boudinaud (Dlle), instit·
J.-F. Pourchier-Vital.
*R. François-Bazin*.
57 *R. François-Bazin*.
59 H. Dianoux. meublé.
Valentin Michel, oiselier·
61 B. Constant·
Joseph Gérardot, employé.
*Boul. d'Athènes* 31.
68 Henri Pascal·
Victor Donadei.
Paul Bayer. employé.
Michel Gallone, voy. de com.
70 *Boul. d'Athènes* 29.

**Donrémy** (rue), du boul. Jeanne-
d'Arc. à la campagne.
(150 m. de long.)
Carré C. 19.

Circonscription électorale : 6me. — Justice de
paix : 6me canton (r. de Bruys 8). — Police :
15e arrond. (boul. Baille 251. — Perception :
7e arr. r. du Coq 17). — Paroisse : St-Pierre·

**Dorade** (r. de la), de la r. St-Christo-
phe 4 à la r. Poissonnerie-Vieille 3.
(33 m. de long.)
Carré H. 10.

Circonscription électorale : 1re. — Just. de
paix : 1er canton (pl. du Mazeau). — Police :
1er arrond. (place Sadi-Carnot 5). — Percep :
1er arrond. (rue de la République 3). —
Paroisse : Saint-Cannat.

5 Alexandre Fiore, comestibles·

**Douane** (tr. de la), du gr. ch. d'Aix
117 à la r. Peyssonnel 22.
(175 m. de long.)
Carré H. 7.

Circonscription électorale : 1re. — Justice de
paix : 3me c. (b. des Dames 27). — Police : 3me
arr. (pl. de Strasbourg 8). — Perc. : 3me
arr. (r. des Dames 68). — Par. : St-Lazare.

2 ......................
6 ......................
10 M. Pinto.

Copiapite

# *Appendix A*

# CHRONOLOGY OF THE ALCHEMICAL REVIVAL

Essential oil

Vinegar

**1786**
Birth of the chemist Chevreul, whose hobby was writing alchemical books

**1805**
Birth of Ferdinand-Marie de Lesseps, builder of the Suez Canal

Glass

**1810**
Birth of the occultist Eliphas Lévi (Abbé Constant, who was only a deacon)

**1814**
Birth of the architect Viollet-le-Duc

Talc

**1819**
Birth of Louis Figuier, well-known historian of alchemy

**1827**
Birth of Marcellin Berthelot, father of thermodynamics

Subacetate of copper

**1828**

Birth of Grasset d'Orcet, philologist and archaeologist, at Cusset; death of Louis-François de Bourbon Cusset, born in 1748 at Cusset

**1830**

Beginning of Auguste Comte's positivist philosophy (from 1830 to 1842)

**1831**

Birth of Héléna Blavatsky; publication of *Notre-Dame-de-Paris* by Victor Hugo

**1832**

Publication of *Hermès Dévoilé* by Cyliani

**1838**

Birth of F. Ch. Barlet (Albert Faucheux)

**1841**

Birth of Schuré

**1842**

Birth of Saint-Yves-d'Alveydre; Tiffereau succeeds in a transmutation in Mexico; birth of Jules Doinel

**1843**

Publication of Cambriel's course in alchemy

**1845**

Beginning of Viollet-le-Duc's restoration work on Notre-Dame Cathedral in Paris; birth of Antoine Dujols de Valois at Saint-Illide, in the Cantal region

**1850**

Publication in England of *A Suggestive Inquiry into the Hermetic Mystery,* by Mary Anne Atwood; birth of Commander Levet in Annecy

**1854**

Publication of *L'Achimie et les Alchimistes* by Louis Figuier

**1856**

Birth of the writer Rosny (senior)

**1857**

Publication of *Histoire de la France Allevysée* by Allévy

**1859**

Birth of Péladan

**1860**

Birth of Oswald Wirth

**1861**

Birth of Stanislas de Guaita; birth of Félix Gaboriau

**1862**

Birth of Pierre Dujols de Valois at Saint-Illide, in the Cantal region

**1865**

Birth of Papus (Gérard Encausse)

**1868**

Birth of Albert Poisson, Jules Bois, and Marc Haven (E. Lalande)

**1871**

Birth of Paul Le Cour and Sédir (Yvon Le Loup); the Paris Commune

**1874**

Birth of Grillot de Givry

**1875**

Birth of the Kabbalist Paul Vulliaud; death of Eliphas Lévi

**1876**

Birth of Jollivet-Castelot at Douai

**1877**

Birth of Jean-Julien Champagne at Levallois-Perret; birth of Raymond Roussel and O. V. de Lubicz Milosz

**1879**

Death of Eugène Viollet-le-Duc

**1880**

Birth of the Hellenist Mario Meunier

**1881**

Birth of J. Bricaud, gnostic bishop

**1886**

Birth of René Guénon

**1887**

Birth of René Schwaller at Asnières

**1888**

Birth of Alexandre Rouhier at Lyons

**1889**

Death of the chemist Chevreul, at age 103

**1891**

Death of Héléna Blavatsky

**1892**

Death of Antoine Dujols de Valois, at age forty-seven

**1893**

Death of Albert Poisson

**1894**

Death of Ferdinand de Lesseps and of Louis Figuier

**1897**

Death of Stanislas de Guaita

**1898**

Birth of Savoret

**1899**

Birth of Eugène Canseliet at Sarcelles

**1900**

Death of Grasset d'Orcet at Cusset

**1902**

Birth of Jules Boucher; death of Jules Doinel

**1905**

Successful transmutation in Paris by Dr. Alphonse Jobert

**1907**

Death of Marcellin Berthelot

**1909**

Death of Saint-Yves-d'Alveydre

**1911**

Death of Félix Gaboriau; death of Commander Levet, at age sixty-three

**1914**

Publication of *Mutus Liber* and *Hypotypose* by Magophon (Pierre Dujols)

**1915**

Death of Abbé Henri Boudet, born in 1837, author of *La Vraie Langue Celtique*

**1916**

Death of Papus

**1917**

Death of Abbé Saunière, born in 1852, who was the curé at Rennes-le-Château

**1918**

Death of Joséphin Péladan

**1919**

Publication of *Voyages en Kaléidoscope* by Irène Hillel-Erlanger

**1920**

Death of Louise Barbe

**1921**

Death of Barlet

**1926**

Publication of *Le Mystère des Cathédrales,* signed by Fulcanelli; death of Pierre Dujols de Valois (in April), at age sixty-four; death of Sédir and of Marc Haven

**1929**

Death of Grillot de Givry and of Schuré

**1930**

Publication of *Les Demeures Philosophales,* signed by Fulcanelli

**1932**

Death of Jean-Julien Champagne (in August), at age fifty-five

**1933**

Death of Raymond Roussel

**1934**

Death of J. Bricaud

**1939**

Death of O. V. de L. Milosz and of Jollivet-Castelot

**1940**

Death of Rosny (senior)

**1943**

Death of Oswald Wirth

**1945**

Death of Phaneg

**1947**

Death of Lucien Faugeron, disciple of Pierre Dujols

**1950**
Death of Paul Vulliaud

**1951**
Death of René Guénon

**1954**
Death of Paul Le Cour

**1957**
Death of Jules Boucher, at age fifty-five

**1960**
Death of Mario Meunier

**1961**
Death of René Schwaller de Lubicz, at age seventy-four

**1968**
Death of Alexandre Rouhier at Bourron

**1977**
Death of Savoret

**1982**
Death of Eugène Canseliet, at age eighty-three

Copiapite

# *Appendix B*

# CHRONOLOGY OF COMMANDER LEVET; LETTER FROM LEVET TO PAPUS

Essential oil

Vinegar

## Chronology of Commander Levet

### June 5, 1850

Levet is born at Annecy (département of Haute-Savoie) as François-Joseph-Aimé-Eugène Levet, son of Antoine-Aimé Levet, director of the Annecy branch of the Banque de France, and Caroline-Albertine Chauvin. He completes secondary school studies at Lycée Impérial Saint-Louis in Paris.

Glass

### 1870

He is appointed to an engineering post on leaving the École Polytechnique.

### 1877

He becomes captain of the 4th Regiment of Engineers, Grenoble.

Talc

### June 4, 1878

He marries Marie-Berthe-Isabelle-Félicie Mialhet de Bessettes, age twenty-three, at Langogne (département of Lozère).

Subacetate of copper

## 1897

He is appointed head of engineering at Constantine, in Algeria.

## 1904

He is appointed head of engineering at Nice, where he begins retirement on October 26. He instructs that his pension be delivered to him in Paris at 19 boulevard Morland (4th arrondissement).

## September 27, 1914

He dies at Bergerac (département of Dordogne), at age sixty-three.

## Letter from Commander Levet to Papus
## (Municipal Library of Lyons; call number 5487;
## Papus Collection)

### Ven ∴ Gr ∴ M ∴ and T ∴ C ∴ F ∴ ,

In a previous letter you conferred upon me the honor of considering me as S ∴ I ∴ in spite of the inadequacy of my qualifications. Please allow me to recall this honor in order to ask you to put me in touch with Martinists who might be living in Constantine or who might be here on a trip and, in spite of the distance from Tunis, with the general representative and the Lodge of Tunis.

I see in the proceedings that you have published (*Initiation*, March 1897) that the general representative in Egypt succeeded in concluding an agreement with the Baha'is of Persia. By means of the hieroglyphics, I understand this order to be an Ionian faction of Islam.

I believe it would be easier and even more advantageous to put the Martinist Order in contact with the Tidjanya and with the Quadrya.

The administration of indigenous affairs in Algeria considers the Tidjanya as devoted friends of the French influence. They seem to have a special veneration for Sidi Aïssa (Jesus) and, like the Albanian Baktachi, can be favorable to Christians. Henri Duveyrier, the explorer of the

Algerian Sahara, was a *khouan* [adherent] of their order. Recently as well Mr. de Brazza made the trip from Laghouat to take from there the *ward* (the rose). Their grand master resides at Tlemcen, near Touggourt, and our division chief never makes the trip without going to see him. I have good reason to believe that the Quadrya would also be very accessible. They are a much more powerful order, much more widespread than the Tidjanya, who are mostly Algerian (Algerian provinces, from Constantine and Tunisia). The Quadrya have their center at Baghdad near the tomb of their patron, Sidi 'Abd al-Qadir Jilani, perhaps the greatest saint of Islam and certainly the best known (almost all the poor beg alms in his name). The emir 'Abd al-Qadir belongs to them. I believe them to be Dorian, however. In contrast, the brotherhoods originating from Morocco all seem to me to be Ionian and hostile.

However it may be, I remain at your disposal for any initiative that might be useful to the order, and I beg you to count on my complete support.

Constantine, May 30, 1897
Commander Levet, Head of Engineering at Constantine

The Moslem brotherhoods have very curious and very interesting prophecies. One of them from the end of the eighteenth century predicted very clearly the conquest of Algeria by the French. I will communicate that to Saturninus.

*Appendix C*

# CHRONOLOGY OF RENÉ SCHWALLER DE LUBICZ

## December 30, 1887

He is born at Asnières in the département of Seine-et-Oise. He spends his childhood and his adolescence in Strasbourg, where his father is a pharmacist-chemist. His father, originally from Switzerland, studied pharmacy in Germany.

## 1910

He arrives in Paris and becomes the student of Matisse. It is here that he meets a very beautiful young woman whom he marries and with whom he has a son. She looks after his painter's studio for him. He comes in contact with the occult milieu of Paris and in particular with the hermetic circle developing around Jean-Julien Champagne. A meeting with Champagne turns into a twenty-year collaboration.

## 1914–18

He is mobilized and assigned to an army laboratory, where he is responsible for carrying out chemical analyses on the feeding of troops. He is already interested in theories about the constitution of matter.

## 1919

The Lithuanian poet Oscar Vladislas de Lubicz Milosz confers on him the right to bear the coat of arms of Lubicz.

## 1920

He creates the association Les Veilleurs and a journal, *Le Veilleur.*

## 1922

He departs for Suhalia in Switzerland, where, with the help of a few faithful friends, he founds a scientific research station.

## 1927

He marries Jeanne Germain, born in 1885 and the widow of Georges Lamy, better known by the mystic name Isha, who participates in all his researches. Prior to her marriage to Schwaller, she bore four children, two daughters and two sons. Tragically, she lost her eldest daughter and her youngest son, Jacques. Her second daughter, Lucie Lamy, becomes the staunch collaborator of Aor, and her son, Jean Lamy, becomes a valued doctor.

## 1929

He purchases the dwelling Les Platanes in Plan-de-Grasse, to which Isha assigns the name Lou-Mas-de-Coucagno. He begins experiments on stained glass with J.-J. Champagne.

## 1930

Champagne and Schwaller find success in these experiments, which Aor relates to Mr. VandenBroeck and which appear in his book, *Al-Kemi, a Memoir: Hermetic, Occult, Political, and Private Aspects of R. A. Schwaller de Lubicz.*

## 1931–32

The final meetings occur between J.-J. Champagne and R. Schwaller. Champagne dies in Paris on August 26, 1932.

**1938**

The Schwaller family settle in Egypt, where they remain for fifteen years, fourteen of which are spent in Luxor. The painter Alexandre Stoppelaere, the architect-archaeologist Clément Robichon, and the archaeologist Alexandre Varille join in Schwaller's research. Together they form the Groupe de Luxor. (In 1937 in Paris, the publisher Paul Harmann had published *En Égypte* by Varille and Robichon.)

**1952**

Schwaller returns to Plan-de-Grasse and publishes many books.

**1961**

On December 7, René Schwaller dies at Plan-de-Grasse.

**1962**

In December, Jeanne Schwaller dies in Paris.

# *Appendix D*

# LETTER FROM RENÉ SCHWALLER TO UNKNOWN RECIPIENT

Copiapite

Essential oil

Vinegar

Glass

Talc

What follows is a typed version of the manuscript draft of a letter from Aor dated 1960.

Dear Sir:

I am indeed very late in replying to the questions in your letter of August 4, and I beg you to excuse this delay.

You are asking quite embarrassing questions, not that I am unable to reply, but what will you make of my explanations? Everything relating to my great brother Milosz and his new orientation since 1917 concerns me and, when simple people are unaware of the causes, they make them up, and rarely are these imaginings favorable—for people are more moved by the bad than by the good. Moreover, people love window dressing in order, shall we say, to make the stupidities pleasanter rather than seeking the bare and simple truth.

As for your questions on esotericism in general, La Colombe will soon release a number on this issue. It will be a pleasure to send you a copy.

Subacetate of copper

Nowadays the atomic age has sprouted so-called alchemists in every direction. Alchemy is often spoken of without realizing that it is not a procedure for making gold, but rather is the echo of a very noble, priestly science bequeathed from antiquity, a science arising from Al-Kemit (pharaonic Egypt) and recorded everywhere, especially on the scrolls of Thot, whom the Greeks called Hermes—which, by the way, is a pharaonic word meaning "birth of Her," or Kor, the Horus of the Romans. Another publication that will be issued, probably in the spring, will attempt to set this straight. I'll let you know about its release.

Certainly it was I who revealed to Milosz the deepest meaning that we must attribute to hermetic science. This radically changed his way of seeing the world, and God knows that at the time I had still much, definitely much, to learn. But the poet never feared getting carried away and he published *Ars Magna,* which I was never happy with. But O. W. de L.-M. was like a fiery horse, impossible to hold back once he had awakened his captivating (?) Olympian dream. If I may be permitted a piece of advice, do not let yourself be taken in by modern writings claiming to be alchemical; they can only lead you astray. This is a very serious problem.

As for Les Veilleurs, I am the chief culprit. In the beginning, in 1917, I had organized meetings the aim of which was solely to provide everyone an opportunity, in a small group, to develop a theme on any subject whatever. Right away the mystical took over and led us to meet only for mystical purposes—to the exclusion of any religious or political critique. When, at the end of the war, my old friend Gaston Revel, founder and editor in chief of the magazine *Le Théosophe,* offered to put this magazine at the service of our group, I proposed calling it *Le Veilleur.* It was in this way that this movement was born—a movement about which people have spoken a great deal but have understood nothing—for one of our aims was to help demobilized craftsmen to find the opportunity to readjust to a new life guided by a sense that was mystic rather than one that was purely economic.

Now all this had no connection whatsoever with the Theosophical Society to which I had belonged from 1913 to 1916. I am infinitely grateful to this movement for having opened my eyes to certain aspects of Buddhism, but later I had to follow my own path.

I am familiar with the explanation of René Guénon about Les Veilleurs and about myself. He was mistaken on several points, particularly about my friendship with Gaston Revel, which remained strong right up until his death in 1939. I have always been direct and frank, and this has allowed me to experience in this life friendships that were impervious to any attack—and equally, a few enemies who were always hidden, acting surreptitiously. Some called me diabolical, others satanic or attributed to me black masses and other stupidities. The Surrealists called me Luciferian, basing this on an essay entitled "Adam, l'homme rouge," which I burned. In 1921, I broke with all these movements: Les Veilleurs, Centre Apostolique, and—from one day to the next—I closed down the paper *Le Veilleur,* which had become a magazine. In general, I never appeared in public. It was to Carlos Larronde—also a great friend of Milosz—that I delegated the task of speaking in public, to which he was perfectly suited.

The last time I saw my great friend Milosz, who more and more took refuge in Catholicism (for personal reasons that I am probably the only one to be acquainted with), was in 1929, when he said to me, in his style that bordered on the whimsical: "Why don't you want to turn Catholic? Then there would be at least two Catholics in the world." Later, he took refuge in a lay order of Trappists. O. W. de Lubicz-Milosz, prince of Lusace, count of Labunovo, head of the Bozawola branch of the Lubicz clan, welcomed me into this clan with the right to the coat of arms and to its titles. What there is that is most precious for me in this affair is to wear the ring with the Lubicz arms, a jewel that belonged to Milosz's father, a constant reminder for me of one of my most sincere and most rewarding friendships. From 1930 on, I sought out isolation, and, giving my new address to only a few friends, I secluded myself here at Plan-de-Grasse and later for two years in Mallorca, in an old hospice from the time of Raymond Lully, then in Egypt, source of all wisdom.

Copiapite

Essential oil

Vinegar

Glass

Talc

Subacetate of copper

# TRANSLATION OF PIERRE DUJOLS'S OBITUARY

For a facsimile of the obituary, see figure 5.15 on page 80.

Mr. Pierre Dujols

This past April 19, Mr. Pierre Dujols died at the age of 64 after several days of suffering and a life that had been physically overwhelming for many years. Mr. Dujols, not well known by the general public, was known to a small circle of people who struggled to penetrate the secrets of hermetic science. In my opinion, Mr. Dujols possessed a body of knowledge in this field that places him at the forefront of those who studied the Kabbalah and hermeticism in modern times.

His extensive learning is evidenced by the catalog of esoteric books that he published before the war in a substantial octavo volume that constitutes a real storehouse of useful information and quality summaries based on the sometimes considerable analysis he devoted to the works being cataloged.

Certain of these cataloged works, sometimes being sold very cheaply, are analyzed with two columns of densely written text. This provides for the scholars as well as for seekers the most precious and useful documentation, for Caillet's dictionary has been limited to only very brief analyses.

The studies by Mr. Dujols on the books he examined were made for his own use and were integrated with the knowledge he had already accumulated. They point out those things that are useful to know in order to develop the initiation that each individual must acquire by his own efforts, and not through the didactic teaching of a group leader. Moreover, he who has, by himself, entered upon the way and who wishes to work on his inner temple will find in these analyses precious directions, for they have come from an initiate. I declare here the wish that this catalog of Mr. Dujols may be gathered together with a listing of the books, organized by the names of the authors, so that it may form a precious document for all seekers.

We might ask, "Why did he write nothing himself? Why did he not put forth his personal synthesis?" Indeed, all we know that is written by him besides these analyses is the preface he wrote to the *Mutus Liber* of Mr. Nourry, a preface that shines with the vast learning, or rather, the "knowledge" that he possessed. He did, however, leave behind a manuscript that he did not think suitable to publish during his lifetime. I do not know if it will be made public, but I do hope that this effort from an entire lifetime not be left forever in darkness.

A disturbing question remains about this elevated personality who has left us: Did he really, as I believe he did, know the secret of the Great Work?

The refinement of his philosophy and certain enigmatic words he let drop would indicate (as my personal conviction indicates) that this man—so detached from a search for glory or fame and of a fundamentally honest nature—was acquainted with the operational method of the Great Work, and if he did not pursue it to its ultimate accomplishment, it was only because he had to suspend his operations by reason of his state of health and by reason of material and financial difficulties.

For those who do not believe in the reality of metallic transmutations but only in a representation of the sublimating operations of the soul, or for those who, like myself, tend not to be so concerned about this issue, he maintained with all his authority that metallic transmutation is possible, that it was known from the most remote antiquity, and that it is knowledge of that alone that can provide the power—a power both sacred and royal—to confer on the initiates the knowledge of the spiritual and material laws of the universe as well as its past and future history.

He took his secret with him, having judged it not good to divulge, even to those who shared his complete confidence, but his life can be an example: Those who truly embark upon the hermetic way must expect, as did he, to meet silence, isolation, solitude, and the lack of understanding of others. There are reasons why the word *hermit* has so many connections with the name Hermes. At the threshold of such a life, the being hesitates and ponders; he cannot conceive that he might, at the same time, have so much knowledge and not be understood. As Christ in the Olive Garden, he is tempted to say: "Father, remove this cup from me." But also like Christ, he cannot avoid entering the *via dolorosa* where there awaits him abandonment by friends, scorn, being spat upon by the ignorant, and the ascension of Calvary up until the moment when finally, for him, the veil of the Temple is rent.

Mr. Pierre Dujols ascended his Calvary and now, for him, no doubt, the Holy of Holies is devoid of mystery.

Copiapite

*Appendix F*

# TRANSLATION OF THE LETTER FROM CANSELIET TO SCHWALLER DE LUBICZ

Essential oil

Vinegar

For a facsimile of the letter, see figure 6.1 on pages, 102–103.

Paris, December 4, 1933

Sir:

Glass

It is possible that my name which appears on the back of the envelope is not entirely unknown to you, for, very connected as you were with Mr. Champagne in the final years of his life, you must have heard him sometimes speak of me. Since his death, I have continued by myself the pursuit of an aim that arose from a collaboration lasting seven years and for which purpose we had rented, in January 1925, two adjoining garrets at 59A rue de Rochechouart. As it happens, I have had the good fortune and the pleasure to receive in the past few days the loan of a very interesting book, *Adam, l'homme rouge,* and to have learned from it what our common friend had failed to tell me:

Talc

Subacetate of copper

141

that you are the author of this curious and scholarly work. You demonstrate profound knowledge at the juncture of the primitive androgynous state, as well as highly philosophical concerns—in fact the same as those that gripped Mr. Champagne upon his return from Plan-de-Grasse and that seemed to overturn his former notions. In conformity with this new orientation, we both engaged once again in the study of *caput mortuum* from the first work, which we had always rejected as useless scoria having no value. No doubt we were wrong about that because numerous philosophers assured us that this material, with its crude aspect and its strong odor, is the *flower of all metals,* the *flos florum,* which they regard so highly. They gave it this name because just as the flower prepares the fruit and as the fruit is virtual in the flower, this earth carries within it the invisible embryo of a new mineral essence. The *Turba Philosophorum* warns us of this in two different places. In one of these, "*Eximiganus* says: Know that our entire primary intention is the *misty Maye jacket*"; in the other reference, "*Theophilus* says: Know, all you sons, of the doctrine that the secret of everything is a *misty covering* of which the Philosophers have so often spoken." Indeed, Avicenna teaches that we must assemble our material consisting of droppings, filth, and rot from the sun and the moon. Some philosophers, in order to characterize the impurity of the magma from which the hermetic lily is born, have given it the name *manure.* The sage knows how to recognize our stone even in the manure, claims the Cosmopolite, whereas the one who is ignorant will not be able to find me in gold.

This is a warning given to the craftsman who might be tempted, within the natural separation or decomposition, to keep the brilliant, the dazzling, the splendid, because it seems to him to be very pure, while despising the residual manure, these feces, "filthy and foul," in the midst of which, however, there rests and hides the best of what he is looking for.

I am continuing, then, the labors of the Great Work in that direction which I have no doubt you would have impressed upon the experimentations of Mr. Champagne. As a result, and especially after reading *Adam l'homme rouge,* I am led to believe that you would have yourself obtained in the laboratory this *alchemical mercury,* this *adamic earth* that is also *Adam, l'homme rouge.* Don't you in fact say, on pages 48 and 49, all the while establishing a striking parallel between these two works, the physico-human and the physico-chemical: "Why these substances: sulfur, salt, and mercury? Because they are as typical as can be. Sulfur, product of the fire of the earth; mercury, the water of metals, or the first earthly body; and salt, the stable state that is most pervasive. On the other hand, sulfur coagulates mercury and forms a *salt that is black* and *red.* We must remember that the Rosicrucian philosophers never took the words *sulfur, salt,* and *mercury* for anything other than symbols of the Trinity. But that is something that the *intellectualized mentality of our present-day science* is scarcely capable of understanding.

"There is a principle that acts, a principle that receives, and the two form, through a mutual love (successive attraction and repulsion from the process of generation), the perfect salt that is *three* in *one:* God in the trinity, called into the material work of the philosophers—the philosopher's stone, the word *stone* here signifying symbolically the perfect form, the most stable, the most material, the most 'formal.' And the modifier *philosopher's* means that it is to be heard in the sense of esoteric knowledge . . . ."

This whole passage, in my mind, constitutes a revelation that is of no small importance.

Similarly, on page 89, we find a very big secret in a little passage: "As for woman, she holds in herself the memory of her decline from man into woman. She cannot become man except by *blending* herself with him. Then the two will no longer be two but an *animated substance.*"

Might it not be that Mr. Champagne has once again shown, with respect to this material aspect of your work, a memory lapse that is as surprising as it is incomprehensible, or else an importunate discretion or perhaps an excessive reserve? Whatever it may be, I have not managed to banish the painful impression that has been left in me by unexpected events, by unsuspected facts, that arose both at the end of his life and after his death and which gave rise to horrible scenes. I scarcely know how to determine whether these scenes were more disgusting than they were painful. I must also say that for a long time, there had arisen unnoticed and had been maintained over him the deplorable domination of a woman—alas, a domination such as that which narrow-minded individuals too often exert over superior minds.

But all that is nothing and is of no interest other than that interest, negligible in itself, which we can attach to the fabricated things of this world. It is a completely different value that I ascribe to the response that you might judge proper to send me in order to enlighten me, insofar as you judge it useful so to do, given the key importance of the great work.

Yours truly,
Eugène Canseliet
10 quai des Célestins
Paris, 4th arrondissement

## *Appendix G*

## CHRONOLOGY OF EUGÈNE CANSELIET (FROM ATORÈNE, *LE LABORATOIRE ALCHIMIQUE*, TRÉDANIEL)

Copiapite

Essential oil

Vinegar

Glass

### 1899

He is born at Sarcelles (département of Val-d'Oise) on Monday, December 18, 8:00 P.M., the son of Eugène-Léon Canseliet. His father, a mason, dies in 1919.

### 1916

He becomes a friend of Jean-Julien Champagne.

### 1917

He obtains his baccalaureate in Latin and Greek literature at Aix-en-Provence.

Talc

### 1920

He is employed in accounting at the gas factory in Sarcelles.

Subacetate of copper

**1921**

On January 15, he marries Raymonde Caillard, age nineteen. Divorce follows.

**1921**

On August 10, his son, Henri; is born. Henri dies seven years later.

**1922**

He attends a transmutation carried out by Fulcanelli at the gas factory in Sarcelles.

**1925**

He moves into a garret at 59A rue de Rochechouart next to Jean-Julien Champagne. In December, the publisher Jean Schémit agrees to publish the manuscript *Le Mystère des Cathédrales,* brought to him by Canseliet.

**1926**

*Le Mystère des Cathédrales* is published in an edition of three hundred copies.

**1927**

On January 3 his daughter, Solange, is born.

**1930**

*Les Demeures Philosophales* is published in an edition of five hundred copies.

**1933**

He moves into a  sixth-floor garret at 10 quai des Célestins.

**1937**

On January 26, he marries Solange's mother, Germaine Raymonde Hubat.

**1938**

He moves into an apartment at Deuil-la-Barre (département of Val-d'Oise) with his whole family. On July 21, his second daughter, Isabelle, is born.

**1939**

He moves with his family to Blicourt, near Beauvais (département of Somme).

**1940**

On December 16, his third daughter, Béatrice, is born.

**1945**

His book *Deux Logis alchimiques* (Two Alchemical Dwellings) is published by Schémit.

**1946**

In June, he goes to live in Savignies, near Beauvais.

**1955**

He translates (and adds his commentary to) *Les Douze Clefs de la philosophie* (The Twelve Keys of Philosophy) by Basile Valentin. It is published in 1956 by Les Éditions de Minuit.

**1964**

*Alchimie* is published by Pauvert.

**1967**

His commentary on *Mutus Liber* is published by Pauvert.

**1972**

*L'Alchimie expliquée sur ses textes classiques* (Alchemy Explained According to Its Classic Texts) is published by Pauvert.

## 1974

He suffers coronary thrombosis and recovers with the aid of the alchemical salt of dew.

## 1975

*Trois Anciens Traités d'Alchimie* (Three Ancient Treatises on Alchemy) is published by Pauvert.

## 1982

Eugène Canseliet dies. He is buried at La Neuville-Vault.

# *Appendix H*

# NATAL CHART OF PIERRE DUJOLS

He was born at Saint-Illide in the Cantal region on March 22, 1862, at 7:00 A.M.

His chart can be summarized as follows:

- 2  trines, 2 squares,
- 2  conjunctions,
- 6  planets out of 10 are unaspected.

The use of 72-degree aspects will facilitate the interpretation of the chart, although their use introduces a difficulty as to the attribution and use of such angles.

We find four such aspects. Three 72-degree aspects mark a personality or a circumstance that is really out of the ordinary, indicating thereby a life that relates to that which is beyond, toward elsewhere, as we might say: the place behind the mirror, the world of unmanifest things and of the unfolding of events.

Classical astrology provides very few indications of the properties of this aspect. On the other hand, it divides the 360-degree circle into five equal parts. There are other seldom used aspects, such as 51 degrees, which divides the zodiac into seven parts and which can therefore be attributed to Libra; or that of 40 degrees, which would reinforce the influence of Jupiter.

The 72-degree aspect is an aspect of Leo. Some authors attribute to it the properties of good fortune, of creation, a sort of *baraka*.

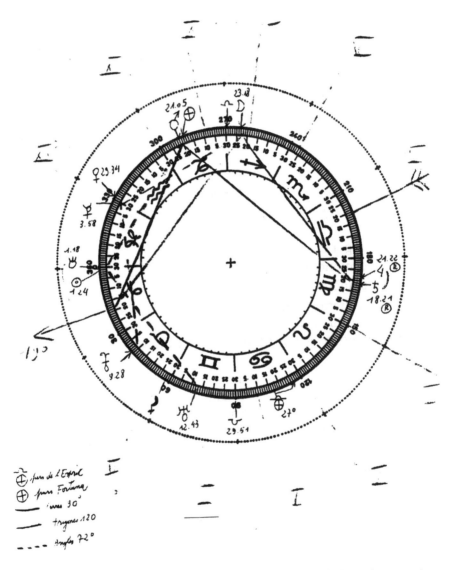

Fig. H.1. *Natal chart of Pierre Dujols, born at Saint-Illide in the Cantal region at 7:00 A.M., March 22, 1862*

The ruler of the chart, the Sun in the present case, is exalted at 1 degree of Aries, but it is in the twelfth house, which portends good fortune, a social success through the intermediary of secret, occult, and hidden facts. But social success and good fortune are limited. This same Sun at 1 degree of Aries is framed by Neptune and Pluto. Pluto is in its detriment in the sign of Taurus. This triptych is the mark of an active search using the imagination. Spiritual or scientific elements can be mixed with this, but in an odd manner. Sometimes the essential is lost sight of. On the emotional side, there coexists the meeting of exceptional individuals with whom one could have chaotic or agonizing relationships. Strong intuition that is not always controlled can lead the person to a conversion or to an art that turns his life upside down.

The Aries Ascendant between the Sun and Pluto is an indicator of strong activity and of convictions bitterly defended. Through Pluto, there is a work and a personality behind the scenes, along with scarcely common endeavors and a constant need to hide a segment of life. This same Pluto is in an aspect of 72 degrees with Venus approaching the twelfth house. That aspect is the indicator of a secret passion governing the existence. Pluto, ruler of the first house in the first house, strengthens the secret goals of the individual and confers on him a power to get to the bottom of things and people. The Sun, ruler of the Ascendant in the twelfth house, conjunct Neptune, predestines, once again, an individual's hiding of himself and at times a self-delusion in spite of an important interior life. It is also the indication of a social life that can be subject to ordeals and illnesses. The individual, however, will rise above that and dominate those around him. Mars is exalted in the sign of Capricorn in the tenth house and predisposes an individual to shine late in life. An aspect of Sun-Uranus in the second house in the sign of Gemini reveals a life of friendships that are intellectually and spiritually rich. There can be friends engaged in occult deeds.

Taurus is in the second house, conjunct the Black Moon. Karma affects material goods. The ruler of this second house, Venus, is on the cusp of the Moon. The second ruler, the Moon, which is squaring Jupiter, with Jupiter itself being retrograde in the sixth house and in Virgo, leads us to think that the wealth of this individual is secret or spiritual and arises essentially from his work. The framing of the Black Moon between Uranus and Pluto can be the mark of health problems, important psychic problems (violent on occasion), and intense upheavals.

The sign of Gemini is in the third house; its ruler Mercury is in the twelfth in Pisces. This is the sign of an intelligence that draws its strength from dreams and faith. There is a marked aesthetic sense and perhaps also a taste for the arts. Inspiration is definitely indicated. Thoughts and writings on religious or occult topics are finely nuanced.

The sign of Cancer is in the fourth house. This gives importance to the end of life. The Moon in Sagittarius in the ninth house squares Jupiter in the sixth, in its detriment and retrograde. Jupiter is also conjunct Saturn; this suggests that the latter part of life is sickly, although spent in higher pursuits, and is undoubtedly laborious.

With the sign of Leo in the fifth house, the ruler in Aries in the twelfth house gives a generous passion in love but leans toward hidden passion.

Virgo is in the sixth house with Saturn and Jupiter conjunct. This individual's life can be devoted to a particular task, but Jupiter in its detriment and retrograde squaring the Moon limits his social recognition and success. Certain digestive or skeletal functions can be affected by chronic conditions. Mercury, ruler of Virgo, suggests a tendency toward a certain isolation.

Libra is in the seventh house. Its rulers are, respectively, in the twelfth house (Venus) and in the sixth (Saturn). This can make for contracts that turn into hardships later on. Saturn is found here in the twelfth house from its place of exaltation. The end of life is strongly marked and affected.

Scorpio is in the eighth house. Its ruler, Mars, is exalted in Capricorn in the tenth. The psychic power of the individual is exalted; this individual can be led to seek or to discover people with powers.

Sagittarius is in the ninth house, which includes the Moon. This suggests a great liveliness of mind and voyages of the imagination. The ruler of the ninth house, Jupiter, is in the third house from its exaltation. There is benefit from things of the mind and from writings on subjects that may be occult or religious. The Moon is in the eighth sign fom its exaltation in Taurus.

Capricorn is in the tenth house, which includes the part of Fortune and Mars exalted, leading the individual toward scientific or library work.

The sign of Aquarius is in the eleventh house. There is an importance attached to friendship and to friends who have financial means—also to friends in positions of authority. Uranus, ruler of Aquarius, is in the second house, aspected by the Sun.

The twelfth house is very full. There we find Venus, Neptune, Mercury, and the Sun. Venus is in the sign of Pisces. Mercury here helps discovery through reasoning based on hidden facts. Venus mitigates the ordeals in part, but Neptune suggests betrayal. The Sun ensures success in private life but a vitality suddenly lessened. Jupiter, ruler of the twelfth in the sixth, presages difficulties in the areas of health and hidden income.

Let us be cautious, however, with this very classical and limited interpretation. We could say that the 72-degree aspects indicate good fortune up to a given point. We could add, in summary, that in spite of an exceptional wisdom, destiny strongly limits the goals of this individual. The taste for the secret is too pronounced, the home inadequate, the income certainly insufficient, freedom is definite but spiritual: in the mind, attained late, and communicated to many. This same part of the mind is in the fourth house in Cancer with its two rulers squared. We also notice the Ascendant at the exact point of exaltation of the Sun at 19 degrees of Aries. We can also say that the house of friendships, the eleventh, is distinguished by two rulers that are squared. There will certainly be rich friends, but the individual is led to serve them intellectually.

As an example of the use of 72-degree aspects, we can note the chart of a transmutation (fig. H.2), that of the gold medallion shown by an adept to the chemist Helvetius. At first glance, any well-informed astrologer will distinguish in it the whole importance that the alchemists attribute to astrology. The gold from transmutations is here understood in its true aim—that of a priestly and theurgic tokening.

Paris, October 14, 1991

François Trojani, author of the alchemical commentary on

*Tarots de Mantegna*, Éditions Seydoux

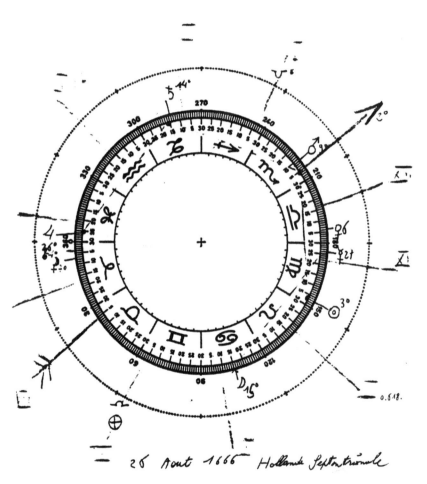

*Fig. H.2. Astrological chart drawn up according to the date inscribed in the medallion of alchemical gold that was worn by Elias Arista, which he showed to the scholar Helvetius. The text accompanying it reads as follows: "From Jehovah. The marvelous and miraculous Knowledge expresses itself in the Holy Book of Nature. I was made August 26, 1666." Chart courtesy of Éditions Traditionelles, Paris.*

# *Appendix I*

# NATAL CHART OF JEAN-JULIEN CHAMPAGNE

Copiapite

Essential oil

Vinegar

Glass

Talc

Champagne was born on January 23, 1877, at 10:00 A.M., at Levallois-Perret. He was an Aquarian by his Sun sign with an Aries Ascendant.

If the natal chart is the structure of the energies of an individual, describing the potentialities that can be developed in the course of his existence and then accomplished, only a direct contact with the individual can inform us about his level of consciousness, his understanding of his own riches, and the integration of his inner conflicts. Given these cautions regarding the use of this chart, the aim of the examination of the chart of Champagne will be, above all, to grasp his essence in its entirety.

Very marked by his solar sign, Aquarius, he is above all an idealist, an innovator, scarcely a conformist, and independent. Deeply touched by the evolution of human beings, he aspires in a brotherly enthusiasm to bring his Promethean contribution to the human race. The presence of the Sun in the eleventh house strengthens his concern for social and collective participation, as well as his desire to widely circulate his knowledge, which is often ahead of its time.

Subacetate of copper

# JEAN-JULIEN CHAMPAGNE

23 JANVIER 1877  10 h
heure TU  9 h 49 mn

LEVALLOIS PERRET
longitude  2°45 E
latitude  48°50 N

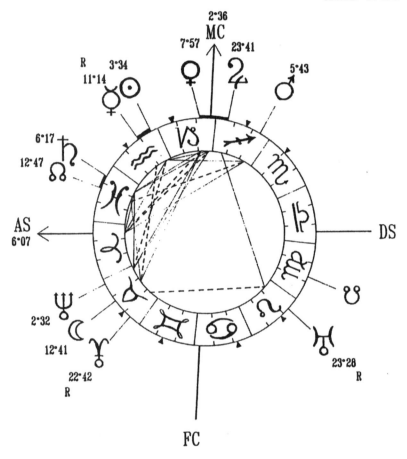

*Fig. I.1. Natal chart of Jean-Julien Champagne*

Another powerful element in his chart, Jupiter in Sagittarius in the ninth house, reinforces humanitarian idealism and the quest for truth. Carried away by an insatiable and boundless thirst for knowledge, in a welcoming attitude of tolerance he always seeks to blend Epicureanism and philosophy, science and spirituality.

He can also be portrayed as a curious gatherer of encyclopedic knowledge. The conjunction of Mercury and the Sun in the sign of Aquarius makes him a very cerebral being, impassioned by reading and writing. He has a quick and inventive mind, is independent in his choices, and, following his personal convictions, cares little for the conventions of his time. With an open and universal intelligence, he multiplies his sources of information, always on the quest for a philosophy of life. The support of Mars in the conjunction of Sun-Mercury makes him pragmatic, an experimenter, a practical and positive soul who loves to plunge into concrete realities, always giving precedence to the application and the utilitarian rather than to pure abstraction. His eagerness to plunge in is equaled only by his impatience.

Being in harmony with his inner life and his private faith and acting from his intuition and his inspiration is the essential mode for an Aries Ascendant having Neptune in the first house. He has courage and audacity and a side that is a bit prophetic. We might even risk describing him as a gentle visionary, a wild romantic with an unstructured life, living at the whim of his reckless humor; he experiences a kind of letting go through a direct contact with the movements of the soul. It is vital for this kind of person to feel himself living intensely, to blend resolutely with the object he contemplates or works upon, totally fixating on his endeavors right up to a complete identification with them.

Letting his imagination wander in the land of ecstasy and prolonging moments of illumination and even of higher consciousness become so imperative that we can easily imagine he is tempted more often than he ought to be by stimulants of all sorts, prolonging through them his subtle madness and delaying the moment of a return to day-to-day reality. As does any individual ahead of his time and far from the daily concerns of his contemporaries, he may often shock, astonish, or disturb those around him as much by his marginal manner of living as by his eccentric clothing.

Only a quest for truth has importance in his eyes. It is this truth that the Ascendant Aries, well aspected by Mars in Sagittarius in the eighth house, pursues wildly, with force and enthusiasm and with no regard for his life or for his health. We must imagine him as a fierce worker, indefatigable, throwing himself as if intoxicated—sometimes even at death's door—into Herculean and dangerous battles. In other words, racing cars might attract him. Through Mars, ruler of the Ascendant in the eighth house, he gives importance only to that which is difficult, that which offers a challenge to be taken up, that in which an exploration calls him.

His sexuality is also passionate, very definitely urgent and obsessive. Always to push farther the limits of sensual pleasure: Is this not the beginning of a spiritual search, the ignition of an opening awareness of the transmutation of energies? This is entirely the symbolism of the eighth house: sexuality as an initiatory death leading to rebirth.

For Champagne, any search can be accompanied only by the integration of energies from "below." Mars makes explicit in his chart this burning desire to explore our dark side in order to bring it to the light, a desire to exorcise this darkness without fear or restraint.

It is now time to broach the great contradiction of the chart, which, as for any overriding tension, seeks out a way to be sublimated in order to ward off a descent into a destructive neurosis that could compromise the stability of the personality.

In this case, there is a contradiction between the sign of Taurus and that of Aquarius: the need of Taurus to be attached to the material and the desire of Aquarius to separate from it. Such is the challenge Champagne is offered if he truly wants to play the role of one who awakens humanity.

Originally, everything is material, and the Moon, in Taurus in this case, incarnates appropriately the original form, the raw material on which all our attachments and all our dependencies are built: voluptuousness of earthly food, unlimited pleasure of the senses, an instinct for owning and keeping. Champagne is very sensitive to this quite acute perception of his incarnation and of the primordial needs that flow from it. He is likely plagued by contradictory demands: taking advantage of the simple pleasures of life, not going beyond the material aspect of things, settling into permanency, and, at the other extreme, giving up all attachments and letting himself be guided by intuition of the ephemeral.

In daily life, the observer can only delight in falling into comical situations that might be generated by incompatible elements. As negligent as this individual might be about his body, he might also have his compulsions about his daily grooming.

If the appearance of his clothing means little to him, he can yet succumb to stylishness in looking for underwear and outfits that have a certain originality, perhaps those unearthed at some secondhand clothing dealer. Venus in Capricorn imparts a taste for antiques, and the good aspect of Venus to the Moon confers on him an undeniable seductive charm that attracts feminine attention—an attention that, of course, he appreciates.

We would be fooling ourselves to think that Champagne is completely uninterested in matters of money. An individual who shares his natal chart has his little deals and tricks, and he may occasionally live out a filching worthy of Harpagon in Molière's *The Miser*. With holes in his pocket some days, ascetic dress on others, he is just as capable of expansive gestures as of scrounging attitudes.

Coming back to the Moon, which is in a strategic position in Champagne's chart, we find it framed by Neptune and Pluto. If Neptune represents a function of dissolution, Pluto represents transformation, a destruction leading to rebirth. With such a framing, matter is accepted in its finite and limited structure. He feels intensely the state of confusion and dissolution of material through the influence of Neptune, the dissociating of its various components. Through the influence of Pluto, the simple identification with material can only be swept away. This is the necessity of destroying matter in order to get to the heart of the atom and then to reconstitute a different, restructured material purged of its flabbiness and imperfection. How can we not see in this insistent torture of matter the whole alchemical process, which begins with the dissolution of matter and seeks its transmutation?

Beyond this alchemical connection, it must be understood how, with Pluto, the sensitivity of Champagne is painful, an ever-present anguish with a poignant feeling of insecurity and exclusion. And his sexuality, as intense as it is, cannot be consummated through his unsatisfied desires and his maniacal drives. How can such an individual find relaxation? Liberating oneself from matter while integrating the invasive shadowy part and making from it an elixir of life: This is the basis of all the creativity in which Champagne was engaged.

This helps us to understand better the whole work on the body and on metals, his interest in the constituent elements of nature and the veneration of forms. Uranus in the sixth house attests to all his qualities as a technician and his truly scientific mind, and Venus finds all her meaning in Capricorn, while seeking sobriety and the delineation of forms.

The Midheaven, place of our social accomplishments, framed by Jupiter and Venus, would lead us to presume this individual's desire for a certain success, an ease in making acquaintances and being noticed, but also a search for appreciation, compliments, honors, and homage accorded to his merits.

In this, too, his fierce desire for independence and for being apart cannot be satisfied by facile exterior indications. This might lead us to expect contradictory and very ambivalent attitudes in his social behavior.

Capricorn in the tenth house and its ruler Saturn in the twelfth house suggest late recognition and posthumous fame.

Saturn in the twelfth house is also, for him, the field of his accomplishment and of his rising above himself: a work of research that is lonely, humble, and laborious, sheltered from curious looks, the choice of an existence that is less glorious and the acceptance of cultivating his own secret garden in silence.

In the twelfth house, the future is prepared, and the individual must understand the importance of guarding his treasures . . . in a word, he must be a sage.

Cast in May 1989
by Véronique Guilet, astrologer, Grenoble

# *Appendix J*

# BIBLIOGRAPHY OF THE WORKS OF RENÉ SCHWALLER DE LUBICZ

## (in order of publication)

*Étude sur les Nombres*. Paris: Librairie de l'Art Indépendant, 1914. English edition, *A Study of Numbers*. Translated by Robert Lawlor. Rochester, Vt.: Inner Traditions, 1986.

———. *Nécessité* (by Aor). Paris: privately printed, 1918.

———. *Adam, l'homme rouge*. Paris: Librairie Stock, 1926.

———. *Le Livre des vivants*. Saint-Moritz: privately printed, 1926.

———. *La Doctrine*. Switzerland: Officina Montalia, 1927.

———. *L'Appel du Feu*. Switzerland: Officina Montalia, 1927.

———. *Le Temple dans l'Homme*. Cairo: Éditions Schindler, 1950. English edition, *The Temple in Man*. Translated by Robert and Deborah Lawlor. Rochester, Vt.: Inner Traditions, 1981.

———. *Du Symbole et de le Symbolique*. Cairo: Éditions Schindler, 1950. English edition, *Symbol and the Symbolic*. Translated by Robert and Deborah Lawlor. Rochester, Vt.: Inner Traditions, 1978.

———. *Le Temple dans l'Homme: Apet Sud à Louqsor, contribution à l'étude de la pensée pharaonique*. Paris: Éditions Caractères, 1957. English edition, *The Temple in Man: Apet of the South*

*at Luxor.* Translated by Deborah Lawlor and Robert Lawlor. Rochester, Vt.: Inner Traditions, 1998.

———. *Propos sur Ésotérisme et Symbole.* Paris: Éditions La Colombe, 1960. English edition, *Esoterism and Symbol.* Translated by André and Goldian VandenBroeck. Rochester, Vt.: Inner Traditions, 1985.

———. *Le Roi de la Théocratie Pharaonique.* Paris: Éditions Flammarion, 1961. English edition, *Sacred Science: The King of Pharaonic Theocracy.* Translated by André and Goldian VandenBroeck. Rochester, Vt.: Inner Traditions, 1982.

———. *Verbe Nature* (dans *"Aor," R. A. Schwaller de Lubicz, sa vie, son oeuvre,* by Isha Schwaller de Lubicz). Paris: Éditions La Colombe, 1963. English edition, *Nature Word.* Translated by Deborah Lawlor. Rochester, Vt.: Inner Traditions, 1990.

———. *Le Miracle Égyptien.* Paris: Éditions Flammarion, 1963. English edition, *The Egyptian Miracle.* Translated by André and Goldian VandenBroeck. Rochester, Vt.: Inner Traditions, 1985.

———. *Les Temples de Karnak.* Paris: Éditions Dervy, 1982. English edition, *The Temples of Karnak.* Photographs by Georges and Valentine de Miré. Translated by Jon Graham. Rochester, Vt.: Inner Traditions, 1999.

———. *Lettres à un disciple.* Paris: Diffusion Traditionnelle, 1990.

*Appendix K*

# A PARTIAL LIST OF BOOKS AND ARTICLES DISCUSSING FULCANELLI

Albertus, Frater [Albert Riedel]. *The Alchemist of the Rocky Mountains*. Salt Lake City: Paracelsus Research Society, 1976.

"Les Alchimistes." *Le Charivari*, no. 16., n.d.

Allieu, B., and B. Lonzième. *Index Général de L'œuvre de Fulcanelli*. Le-Mesnil-Saint-Denis: B. Allieu, 1992.

Amadou, Robert. *Le Feu du Soleil: Entretien sur l'alchimie avec Eugène Canseliet*. Paris: Jean-Jacques Pauvert, 1978.

———. "L'Affaire Fulcanelli." *L'Autre Monde*, nos. 74, 75, 76 (September–November 1983).

Ambelain, Robert. "Dossier Fulcanelli." *Les Cahiers de la Tour-Saint-Jacques*, no. 9. Paris, 1962.

———. *Astrologie Ésotérique*. Paris: Éditions Niclaus, n.d.

Atorène. *Le Laboratoire Alchimique*. Paris: Guy Trédaniel, 1981.

Bechtel, Guy. "Entretien avec Eugène Canseliet sur Fulcanelli, suivi du Mystère Fulcanelli." Privately printed. Blocmgracht, Amsterdam: Bibliotheca Philosophica Hermetica, 1974.

Boucher, Jules. "La Croix d'Hendaye." *Consolation*, nos. 26 and 37 (February 13 and April 30, 1936).

Canseliet, Eugène. *Alchimie*. Paris: Jean-Jacques Pauvert, 1964.

———. *L'Alchimie expliquée sur ses textes classiques*. Paris: Jean-Jacques Pauvert, 1972.

———. *L'Alchimie et son livre muet (Mutus Liber)*. Paris: Jean-Jacques Pauvert, 1967.

———. *Deux Logis alchimiques*. Paris: Jean-Jacques Pauvert, 1979.

———. *Trois Anciens Traités d'alchimie*. Paris: Jean-Jacques Pauvert, 1975.

———. "Les Argonautes et la Toison d'Or." *Atlantis,* no. 66 (July 21, 1935).

Coia-Gatie, A. Preface to Irène Hillel-Erlanger, *Voyages en kaléidoscope*. Paris: Éditions La Table d'Émeraude, 1984.

Cor-Lux, André-Michel. "Lueurs sur *Le Mystère des Cathédrales*." *Initiation et Science,* no. 46 (December 1958).

Courjeaud, Frédéric. *Fulcanelli: Une Identité révélée*. Paris: C. Vigne, 1996.

"Fulcanelli: Hypothèses et réflexions d'un ami de l'Étoile Polaire." *Initiation et Science* (June 1962).

Geyraud, Pierre. *L'Occultisme à Paris*. Paris: Éditions Paul, 1953.

Grasset d'Orcet. Preface to *Matériaux Cryptographiques*. Collected and assembled by Bernard Allieu and A. Barthélémy, 1979.

Johnson, Kenneth Rayner. *The Fulcanelli Phenomenon*. Jersey: Neville Spearman, 1980.

Khaitzine, Richard. *Fulcanelli et le Cabaret du Chat Noir: Histoire artistique, politique et secrète de Montmartre*. Villeselve, France: Ramuel, 1997.

Marly, Claude. "Le Langage secret des cathédrales." *Tout Savoir,* no. 74 (July 1959).

Martínez Otero, Luis Miguel. *Fulcanelli: Una Biografía Imposible*. Barcelona: Éditions Obelisco, 1986.

———. *Fulcanelli: Une Biographie impossible*. Paris: Éditions Arista, 1989.

Pauwels, Louis, and Jacques Bergier. *Le Matin des Magiciens*. Paris: Gallimard, 1960. English edition, *The Morning of the Magicians*. Translated by Rollo Myers. London: Neville Spearman, 1963.

Pradel, Jacques. "Entretien avec Eugène Canseliet." In *Question de . . . ,* no. 51 (1983).

Solazaref. "Les Bûchers du XXe siècle." *Aux Amoureux de Science* (March 1988).

*La Tourbe des Philosophes*. Paris: Éditions La Table d'Émeraude.

VandenBroeck, André. *Al-Kemi, a Memoir: Hermetic, Occult, Political, and Private Aspects of R. A. Schwaller de Lubicz*. Rochester, Vt., and Great Barrington, Mass.: Inner Traditions/Lindisfarne Press, 1987.

Van Lennep, Jacques. *Alchimie*. Paris: Éditions Dervy, 1984.

Weidner, Jay, and Vincent Bridges. *The Mysteries of the Great Cross at Hendaye: Alchemy and the End of Time*. Rochester, Vt.: Destiny Books, 2003.

d'Ygé, Claude. Article in *Initiation et Science,* no. 44 (September and December 1957).

# NOTES

### Foreword

1. Fulcanelli, *Le Mystère des Cathédrales*, translated by Mary Sworder (Suffolk, U.K.: Neville Spearman, 1971). French editions: 1926, 1957, 1964.

2. Fulcanelli, *Dwellings of the Philosophers,* translated by Brigitte Donvez and Lionel Perrin (Boulder, Colo.: Archive Press and Communications, 1999). French editions of *Les Demeures Philosophales:* 1930, 1960, 1977.

3. Eugène Canseliet, *Alchimie expliquée sur les textes classiques* (Paris: Jean-Jacques Pauvert, 1972).

4. Claude Lablatinière d'Ygé, *Nouvelle Assemblée des philosophes chymiques* (Paris: Éditions Dervy, 1954).

5. "Épistola Hermetica V," *Atlantis,* no. 291 (1977).

### Chapter 1

1. Dom A. J. Pernety, *Dictionnaire Mytho-Hermétique* (Paris, 1758); republished by Arché (Milan, 1971). Also, ibid., *Fables Égyptiennes et Grecques* (Paris, 1786); republished by La Table d'Émeraude (Paris, 1982).

2. Abbé Nicolas Lenglet-Dufresnoy, *Histoire de la Philosophie Hermétique* (Paris: Coustelier, 1742).

3. Etteila, *Sept Nuances de l'Oeuvre Philosophique* (n.p., 1785)

4. Bernard Husson, *Deux Traités alchimiques du XIXe siècle* (Paris: Omnium Littéraire, 1964), including L.-P.-F. Cambriel, *Hermès Dévoilé* and *Cours de Philosophie Hermétique.*

5. Anonymous, *Hermès Dévoilé, dédié à la Postérité* (Paris: Félix Locquin, 1832).

6. Related in Jacques Sadoul, *Le Grand Art de l'alchimie* (Paris: J'ai Lu no. 329, 1973), and C. Burland, *Le Savoir caché des alchimistes* (Paris: R. Laffont, 1967).

## Chapter 2

1. See Stanislas de Guaita, *La Clef de la Magie Noire* (Paris: Éditions Durville, 1920).

2. Oswald Wirth, *Le Symbolisme hermétique dans ses rapports avec l'architecture et la Franc-Maçonnerie* (Paris, 1931); Stanislas de Guaita, *L'Occultisme vécu* (Paris, 1935).

3. Fulcanelli, *Les Demeures Philosophales,* vol. 1 (Paris: Édition Pauvert, 1965), chapter 2, regarding Louis d'Estissac, and page 246, regarding the letter *X.*

4. Anatole France, *La Rôtisserie de la Reine Pédauque* (Paris: Calmann-Lévy, 1921). Published in English as *At the Sign of the Reine Pedauque* (New York: Dodd Mead, 1923); Montfaucon de Villars, *Le Comte de Gabalis ou entretiens sur les Sciences Secrètes* (Paris: Éditions La Colombe, 1961).

5. Louis Figuier, *L'Alchimie et les alchimistes* (Paris: Hachette, 1854).

6. Grillot de Givry, *Le Musée des Sorciers, Mages et Alchimistes* (Paris: Éditions Henri Veyrier, 1966).

7. On this topic, see the book by Philippe Encausse about his father, *Papus* (Paris: Éditions Belfond, 1979).

8. *Sectes et sociétés secrètes aujourd'hui . . .* (Paris: Éditions Lefeuvre, 1980).

9. Anonymous, H.B. of L., *Textes et documents secrets de la Hermetic Brotherhood of Luxor* (Milan: Arché, 1988).

10. Ibid.

11. P. B. Randolph, *Magia Sexualis* (Sexual Magic; Paris: Guy le Prat, 1969).

12. Juan Garcia Font, *Histoire de l'Alchimie en Espagne* (Paris: Dervy, 1980); Spanish edition (Madrid: Nacional, 1976).

13. Charles-André Gilis, *Introduction à l'Enseignement et au Mystère de René Guénon* (Paris: Éditions de l'Oeuvre, 1985).

14. Pierre Geyraud, *L'Occultisme à Paris* (Paris: Émile Paul, 1953).

15. Grillot de Givry, *Le Grand Oeuvre* (Paris: Éditions Traditionnelles, 1978).

16. Fondation Dina, Head Office: 170 rue Nationale, 75013 Paris, telephone: 01-45-84-51-57.

## Chapter 3

1. Jacques Van Lennep, *Alchimie* (Paris: Éditions Dervy, 1984).

2. Esprit Gobineau de Montluisant, *Explication très curieuse des énigmes et figures hiéroglyphiques, physiques, qui sont au grand portail de l'Église Cathédrale et Métropolitaine de Notre-Dame-de-Paris.* Eugène Canseliet provided this document for us along with two others in his book *Trois Anciens Traités d'alchimie* (Paris: Jean-Jacques Pauvert, 1975).

## Chapter 4

1. *La Vie Simple de René Guénon* (Paris: Éditions Traditionnelles, 1982).

2. "L'Ère du Verseau," *Charivari,* no. 10 (spring and summer 1970).

3. Georges Ranque, *La Pierre Philosophale* (Paris: Laffont, 1972).

4. Eugène Canseliet, *Feu du Soleil* (Paris: Pauvert, 1978); *L'Alchimie expliquée sur ses textes classiques.*

5. Fulcanelli, *Les Demeures Philosophales,* 3rd edition, vol. 2 (Paris: Pauvert, 1977), chapter on the hermetic cabala.

6. Bernard Husson provides this information in his book *Deux Traités alchimiques du XIXe siècle,* 50, in a footnote.

7. Magophon, *Le Livre d'Images sans Paroles (Mutus Liber),* (Paris: Librairie Nourry, 1914).

8. Antoine Dujols de Valois, *Valois contre Bourbons, simples éclaircissements avec pièces justificatives par un descendant des Valois* (Marseilles: Imprimerie Commerciale Thomas et Cie, 1879).

9. See appendix B for a chronology of Levet.

10. See Brother Francisco Colonna, *Le Songe de Poliphile, ou Hypnérotomachie* (Geneva: Éditions Slatkine, 1981).

11. Pierre Borel, *Trésor des Recherches et Antiquités Gauloises et Françaises* (Paris, 1655).

## Chapter 5

1. René Schwaller, *Étude sur les Nombres* (Paris: Bailly, 1917). Republished in 1979 by Éditions Lauzeray, which no longer exists.

2. Eugène Canseliet, *Deux Logis alchimiques* (Paris: Éditions Pauvert, 1979), 20.

3. Robert Ambelain, *L'Abbé Julio* (Paris: Éditions Vermet, 1981).

4. See Betty J. Teeter Dobbs, *Les Fondements de l'Alchimie de Newton ou la chasse au lion vert* (Paris: Guy Trédaniel, 1981). Translated from the English. Original English title: *The Foundations of Newton's Alchemy, or "The Hunting of the Greene Lyon"* (Cambridge: Cambridge University Press, 1983).

5. Canseliet, *L'Alchimie expliquée sur ses textes classiques,* 40.

6. *Voyages en kaléidoscope,* Irène Hillel-Erlanger, introduction and notes by Jean Laplace (Paris: Éditions de la Tourbe, 1977). Another edition appeared in 1984 from Éditions de la Table d'Émeraude, with a remarkable preface by Mr. Coia-Gatie.

7. Ferdinand de Lesseps, "Trente Ans de ma vie," *Nouvelle Revue* (1887).

8. *Milosz en quête du Divin* [Milosz Questing for the Divine] by Jacques Buge, Librairie Nizet, Paris, 1963.

9. Pierre Mariel, *Dictionnaire des Sociétés Secrètes* (C.A.L., 1971).

10. Saint-Yves d'Alveydre, *Mission des Juifs,* Paris: Calman Lévy, 1884), republished many times and *L'Archéomètre* (Dorbon, 1911). See the excellent bibliography of Saint-Yves d'Alveydre's works in the book by Jean Saunier, *Saint-Yves d'Alveydre, ou une synarchie sans énigme* (Paris: Dervy, 1981).

11. Isha is a recognized author; her works include *Her-Bak, "Pois Chiche"* (Paris: Flammarion, 1955), English edition, *Her-Bak: The Living Face of Ancient Egypt,* translated by Charles Edgar Sprague (Rochester, Vt.: Inner Traditions, 1978); *Her-Bak Disciple* (Paris: Flammarion, 1956), English edition, *Her-Bak, Egyptian Initiate*, translated by Ronald Fraser (Rochester, Vt.: Inner Traditions,

1978); *L'Ouverture du Chemin* (Paris: Caractères, 1957), English edition, *The Opening of the Way: A Practical Guide to the Wisdom Teachings of Ancient Egypt* (Rochester, Vt.: Inner Traditions, 1981); *La Lumière du Chemin* (Paris: La Colombe, 1960), English edition, *Journey into the Light: The Three Principles of Man's Awakening,* translated by Susan D. Resnick (Rochester, Vt.: Inner Traditions, 1984).

12. These facts come from an article by Robert Amadou appearing in *L'Autre Monde* (1983).

13. Soon to be published: *Croquis des Caissons Alchimiques du Château de Dampierre sur Boutonne.* Published by the authors, C. and D. Dumolard, 4 rue de la Liberté, 38000 Grenoble.

14. André VandenBroeck, *Al-Kemi, a Memoir: Hermetic, Occult, Political, and Private Aspects of R. A. Schwaller de Lubicz* (Rochester, Vt., and Great Barrington, Mass.: Inner Traditions/Lindisfarne Press, 1987), 74.

15. See Lamy's *Acupuncture: Phonophorèse, technique-clinique* (Paris: Maloine, 1967).

16. See VandenBroeck, *Al-Kemi,* 190.

17. *Les Demeures Philosophales et le Symbolisme Hermétique dans Ses Rapports avec l'Art Sacré et l'Ésotérisme du Grand Oeuvre,* 2 vols. (Paris: Jean Schémit, 1930), with a preface by Eugène Canseliet, F.C.H. Text illustrated with forty plates based on drawings by Julien Champagne.

18. *Le Temple de l'Homme: Apet Sud à Louqsor, contribution à l'étude de la pensée pharaonique* (Paris: Éditions Caractères, 1957); English edition, *The Temple of Man: Apet of the South at Luxor,* translated by Deborah Lawlor and Robert Lawlor (Rochester, Vt.: Inner Traditions, 1998).

## Chapter 6

1. Pierre Geyraud, *L'Occultisme à Paris* (Paris: Éditions Émile-Paul-Frères, 1953).

2. Claude Seignolle, *Invitation au château de l'étrange—témoignages inédits* (Paris: Éditions Maisonneuve et Larose, 1969).

3. Amadou, *Feu du Soleil,* 122, 121, 129.

4. Kenneth Rayner Johnson, *The Fulcanelli Phenomenon* (Jersey: Neville Spearman, 1980).

5. Miss Moberly and Miss Jourdain, *Les Fantômes de Trianon* (Paris: Éditions du Rocher, 1959), with a preface by Jean Cocteau and an introduction by Robert Amadou.

Coptapite

Essential oil

Vinegar

Glass

Talc

Subacetate of copper

# INDEX

Note: Page numbers in italics
refer to figures in the text.

# Books of Related Interest

**The Mysteries of the Great Cross of Hendaye**
Alchemy and the End of Time
*by Jay Weidner and Vincent Bridges*

**Esoterism and Symbol**
*by R. A. Schwaller de Lubicz*

**Sacred Science**
The King of Pharaonic Theocracy
*by R. A. Schwaller de Lubicz*

**The Temple of Man**
*by R. A. Schwaller de Lubicz*

**The Hermetic Tradition**
Symbols and Teachings of the Royal Art
*by Julius Evola*

**The Mystery Traditions**
Secret Symbols and Sacred Art
*by James Wasserman*

**The Occult Conspiracy**
Secret Societies—Their Influence and Power in World History
*by Michael Howard*

**Walkers Between the Worlds**
The Western Mysteries from Shaman to Magus
*by Caitlín and John Matthews*

Inner Traditions • Bear & Company
P.O. Box 388
Rochester, VT 05767
1-800-246-8648
www.InnerTraditions.com

Or contact your local bookseller